TEACHER'S PET PUBLICATIONS

LITPLAN TEACHER PACK
for
That Was Then, This is Now
based on the book by
S. E. Hinton

Written by
Barbara M. Linde, MA Ed.

© 1997 Teacher's Pet Publications
All Rights Reserved

This **LitPlan** for S. E. Hinton's
That Was Then, This Is Now
has been brought to you by Teacher's Pet Publications, Inc.

Copyright Teacher's Pet Publications 1997
11504 Hammock Point
Berlin MD 21811

Only the student materials in this unit plan may be reproduced. Pages such as worksheets and study guides may be reproduced for use in the purchaser's classroom. For any additional copyright questions, contact Teacher's Pet Publications.

www.tpet.com

TABLE OF CONTENTS *That Was Then, This Is Now*

Introduction	5
Unit Objectives	7
Unit Outline	8
Reading Assignment Sheet	9
Study Questions	13
Quiz/Study Questions (Multiple Choice)	23
Pre-Reading Vocabulary Worksheets	43
Lesson One (Introductory Lesson)	57
Nonfiction Assignment Sheet	60
Oral Reading Evaluation Form	67
Writing Assignment 1	68
Writing Evaluation Form	69
Writing Assignment 2	72
Extra Writing Assignments/Discussion ?s	80
Writing Assignment 3	89
Vocabulary Review Activities	90
Unit Review Activities	91
Unit Tests	97
Vocabulary Resource Materials	129
Unit Resource Materials	145

A FEW NOTES ABOUT THE AUTHOR
S. E. HINTON

Hinton, S. E. (Susan Eloise Hinton) (born 1950), U. S. author, born in Tulsa, Oklahoma, in 1950. As a young writer, Hinton decided to write under her initials in order to deflect attention from her gender. She set out to write about the difficult social system that teenagers create among themselves. Her books struck a chord with readers who saw in her characters many elements of this system that existed in their own schools and towns.

In 1967, while she was still in high school, Hinton published her first book, *The Outsiders*. The story of confrontation between rival groups of teenagers was immediately successful with critics and young readers, and it won several awards. There was some controversy about the level of violence in the novel and in her other works, but Hinton was praised for her realistic and explosive dialogue. The success of *The Outsiders* enabled Hinton to continue her education in college.

She graduated from the University of Tulsa in 1970. Her other novels for young adults include *That Was Then, This Is Now* (1971), *Rumblefish* (1975), *Tex* (1979), and *Taming the Star Runner* (1988). Each of Hinton's books featured a cast of characters that suffered from society's ills. Young people alienated from their families and from their peers were seen to veer into criminal paths. Several of her books, including *Tex, The Outsiders*, and *Rumblefish*, were made into movies.

Courtesy of Compton's Learning Company

INTRODUCTION

This unit has been designed to develop students' reading, writing, thinking, listening and speaking skills through exercises and activities related to *That Was Then, This Is Now* by S. E. Hinton. It includes twenty lessons, supported by extra resource materials.

The **introductory lesson** introduces students to one main theme of the novel *That Was Then, This Is Now* through a discussion activity. Following the introductory activity, students are given an explanation of how the activity relates to the book they are about to read.

The **reading assignments** are approximately twenty pages each; some are a little shorter while others are a little longer. Students have approximately 15 minutes of pre-reading work to do prior to each reading assignment. This pre-reading work involves reviewing the study questions for the assignment and doing some vocabulary work for 5 to 10 vocabulary words they will encounter in their reading.

The **study guide questions** are fact-based questions; students can find the answers to these questions right in the text. These questions come in two formats: short answer or multiple choice. The best use of these materials is probably to use the short answer version of the questions as study guides for students (since answers will be more complete), and to use the multiple choice version for occasional quizzes. It might be a good idea to make transparencies of your answer keys for the overhead projector.

The **vocabulary work** is intended to enrich students' vocabularies as well as to aid in the students' understanding of the book. Prior to each reading assignment, students will complete a two-part worksheet for approximately 8 to 10 vocabulary words in the upcoming reading assignment. Part I focuses on students' use of general knowledge and contextual clues by giving the sentence in which the word appears in the text. Students are then to write down what they think the words mean based on the words' usage. Part II gives students dictionary definitions of the words and has them match the words to the correct definitions based on the words' contextual usage. Students should then have an understanding of the words when they meet them in the text.

After each reading assignment, students will go back and formulate answers for the study guide questions. Discussion of these questions serves as a **review** of the most important events and ideas presented in the reading assignments.

After students complete extra discussion questions, there is a **vocabulary review** lesson which pulls together all of the separate vocabulary lists for the reading assignments and gives students a review of all of the words they have studied.

Following the reading of the book, two lessons are devoted to the **extra discussion questions/writing assignments**. These questions focus on interpretation, critical analysis and personal response, employing a variety of thinking skills and adding to the students' understanding of the novel. These questions are done as a **group activity**. Using the information they have acquired so far through individual work and class discussions, students get together to further examine the text and to brainstorm ideas relating to the themes of the novel.

The group activity is followed by a **reports and discussion** session in which the groups share their ideas about the book with the entire class; thus, the entire class gets exposed to many different ideas regarding the themes and events of the book.

There are three **writing assignments** in this unit, each with the purpose of informing, persuading, or having students express personal opinions. The first assignment is to **inform**: students will write a news article about one event from the novel. The second assignment is to **persuade**: students will persuade one of the characters to change an action. The third assignment is to express a personal **opinion**: students will give their opinion on Bryon reporting Mark to the police.

In addition, there is a **nonfiction reading assignment**. Students are required to read a piece of nonfiction related in some way to *That Was Then, This Is Now*. After reading their nonfiction pieces, students will fill out a worksheet on which they answer questions regarding facts, interpretation, criticism, and personal opinions. During one class period, students make **oral presentations** about the nonfiction pieces they have read. This not only exposes all students to a wealth of information, it also gives students the opportunity to practice **public speaking**.

The **review lesson** pulls together all of the aspects of the unit. The teacher is given four or five choices of activities or games to use which all serve the same basic function of reviewing all of the information presented in the unit.

The **unit tes**t comes in two formats: all multiple choice-matching-true/false or with a mixture of matching, short answer, and composition. As a convenience, two different tests for each format have been included.

There are additional **support materials** included with this unit. The **unit resource section** includes suggestions for an in-class library, crossword and word search puzzles related to the novel, and extra vocabulary worksheets. There is a list of **bulletin board ideas** which gives the teacher suggestions for bulletin boards to go along with this unit. In addition, there is a list of **extra class activities** the teacher could choose from to enhance the unit or as a substitution for an exercise the teacher might feel is inappropriate for his/her class. **Answer keys** are located directly after the **reproducible student materials** throughout the unit. The student materials may be reproduced for use in the teacher's classroom without infringement of copyrights. No other portion of this unit may be reproduced without the written consent of Teacher's Pet Publications, Inc.

UNIT OBJECTIVES *That Was Then, This Is Now*

1. Through reading *That Was Then, This Is Now* students will analyze characters and their situations to better understand the themes of the novel.

2. Students will demonstrate their understanding of the text on four levels: factual, interpretive, critical, and personal.

3. Students will practice reading aloud and silently to improve their skills in each area.

4. Students will enrich their vocabularies and improve their understanding of the novel through the vocabulary lessons prepared for use in conjunction with it.

5. Students will answer questions to demonstrate their knowledge and understanding of the main events and characters in *That Was Then, This Is Now.*

6. Students will practice writing through a variety of writing assignments.

7. The writing assignments in this are geared to several purposes:
    a. To check the students' reading comprehension
    b. To make students think about the ideas presented by the novel
    c. To make students put those ideas into perspective
    d. To encourage critical and logical thinking
    e. To provide the opportunity to practice good grammar and improve students' use of the English language.

8. Students will read aloud, report, and participate in large and small group discussions to improve their public speaking and personal interaction skills.

UNIT OUTLINE *That Was Then, This Is Now*

1 Unit Intro Distribute Unit Materials Non-Fiction Assignment	2 Minilesson: Plot Development PVR Chapter 1	3 ?? Chapter 1 PVR Chapter 2 Minilesson: Conflict	4 ?? Chapter 2 PVR Chapter 3 Oral Reading Evaluation	5 ?? Chapter 3 Writing Assignment #1 Inform
6 Minilesson: Plot PVR Chapter 4	7 ?? Chapters 4-5 PVR Chapter 6 ?? Chapter 6	8 Quiz Chapters 1-6 Writing Conferences PVR Chapter 7	9 ?? Chapter 7 Writing Assignment #2 Persuade	10 Minilesson: Figurative Language PVR Chapters 8-9
11 ?? Chapters 8-9 PVR Chapters 10-11	12 ?? Chapters 10-11 Minilesson: Character Traits	13 Minilesson: Plot Plot Profile	14 Extra Discussion Questions	15 Writing Assignment #3 Personal Opinion
16 Vocabulary Review	17 Unit Review	18 Test	19 Non-Fiction Assignment Presentations	20 Movie

Key: P = Preview Study Questions   V = Vocabulary Work   R = Read

READING ASSIGNMENT SHEET
That Was Then, This Is Now

Date to be Assigned	Chapters	Completion Date
	Chapters 1	
	Chapter 2	
	Chapter 3	
	Chapters 4-5	
	Chapter 6	
	Chapter 7	
	Chapters 8-9	
	Chapters 10-11	

STUDY QUESTIONS

SHORT ANSWER STUDY QUESTIONS *That Was Then, This Is Now*

Chapter 1
1. What was Bryon's problem at the bar? How did he solve it?
2. Where did Mark live, and why?
3. How does Bryon describe the relationship between him and M?
4. Describe M&M.
5. What 'talent' did Mark have, and what happened to him because of it?
6. Why did Curly have a grudge against B?
7. What did M&M say when Mark said he wanted to find someone to jump?
8. Where did Mark and Bryon get the money to pay Charlie?

Chapter 2
1. Where was Bryon's mother, and why?
2. How did Bryon describe himself and Mark?
3. Who was Randy? What did he do for the boys?
4. Whom did Bryon's mother ask him to visit? What did Bryon learn about this person?
5. Bryon said he had never been able to accept something. What was it?
6. Describe Bryon's first meeting with Cathy.
7. What was Mark's opinion of Mike? Who else had this opinion of Mike?

Chapter 3
1. Charlie said Bryon was honest in most ways, except one. In what area was Bryon dishonest? What was Bryon's answer to Charlie's comment?
2. How did Bryon feel about Curtis, and why? What did Mark say the reason was?
3. How did M&M's father treat him? What was Cathy's opinion of this treatment?
4. What did Cathy say about Mark at the dance? What was Bryon's reaction?
5. Describe the incident involving Mark. What happened, and why? What did Bryon do?
6. How did the date with Cathy end?

Chapters 4-5
1. How did Bryon and Mark spend the afternoon?
2. How did people at school feel about the fight?
3. Describe Bryon's mood on Monday.
4. Describe the incident with the principal's car.
5. What was Bryon's main problem about Cathy?
6. Mark and Bryon hustled two men in the bar. What happened after they left the bar? Include all details, in order.
7. True or False: Bryon bought Charlie's car.
8. Who understood how Bryon felt, Cathy or Mark?
9. Bryon said Mark was acting strange. What was he doing?

Short Answer Study Questions *That Was Then*

Chapter 6
1. What happened to the Texans?
2. How did Bryon feel about the sentence the Texans got?
3. Cathy said there were problems at home with M&M. What were they?
4. How did Bryon say he felt about Cathy?
5. What was The Ribbon, and what did Cathy, Mark, and Bryon do there?
6. What did M&M do while they were at The Ribbon?

Chapter 7
1. What was Mr. Carlson's reaction to the news about his son? What did Cathy think?
2. Where did Bryon get a job? What did he change to keep it?
3. Describe Mark and Bryon's meeting with Angela. Retell the events in order. Tell why the incident happened.
4. Bryon said he knew why everyone wanted to be Mark's friend. What was the reason?
5. How did Bryon find where M&M was?
6. Retell the story Mark told about his parents.
7. Bryon told Mark he couldn't help something. What was it?

Chapters 8-9
1. Where did Bryon and Mark go to look for M&M? Did they find him?
2. What did Bryon and Mark discuss when they left the place?
3. What happened to Bryon while he was waiting on the steps at Terry Jones's house?
4. Did Bryon want to get even?
5. How did Mark feel about what happened to Bryon?
6. Mark said he had never worried about something before. What was it?
7. Did Bryon and Mark understand each other's opinions?
8. Where did Bryon go, alone, when he got better? What did he do there?
9. Where did Bryon and Cathy go? What did they find? What did they do about it?

Chapters 10-11
1. What did Mr. Carlson tell Bryon? How did Bryon feel about it?
2. Bryon said something was getting easier. What was it?
3. What did Bryon find when he looked for Mark's cigarettes? What did he do after he found it?
4. What did Bryon tell Mark when he got home? What was Mark's reaction?
5. What did Bryon's mother say when she heard what had happened?
6. What punishment did Mark receive? Why did the judge give him that punishment?
7. What happened to M&M?
8. What happened to Bryon and Cathy?
9. Describe the last meeting between Bryon and Mark.
10. How did Bryon feel at the end of the story?

ANSWER KEY: SHORT ANSWER STUDY QUESTIONS *That Was Then*

Chapter 1

1. What was Bryon's problem at the bar? How did he solve it?
    He already had three dollars of unpaid charges at the bar, and the bartender would not give him credit for another Coke. The bartender threatened to beat Bryon if he didn't pay up by the end of the month. Mark promised to pay the next day, so Charlie let them have their Cokes.

2. Where did Mark live, and why?
    He lived with Bryon and his mother. Mark's parents had shot and killed each other several years earlier, when he was 9 and Bryon was 10, and Mark had lived with them ever since.

3. How does Bryon describe the relationship between him and Mark?
    They are like brothers. They have been friends for years, even before Mark came to live at Bryon's house.

4. Describe M&M.
    M&M was thirteen. He was very serious, with a wide-eyed, trusting look on his face. He had grey eyes and long, charcoal colored hair. He wore an old army jacket, moccasins, and a peace symbol around his neck. He got his nickname because he ate M&M candies constantly.

5. What 'talent' did Mark have, and what happened to him because of it?
    He could hot-wire anything, and had been caught stealing a car. Now he was on probation, and had to see the probation officer weekly.

6. Why did Curly have a grudge against B?
    Bryon used to go with Curly's sister. She broke up with him, but he spread it around school that he broke up with her.

7. What did M&M say when Mark said he wanted to find someone to jump?
    He said they made him sick. They had just saved him from being jumped, and now they were going to do the same thing to someone else.

8. Where did Mark and Bryon get the money to pay Charlie?
    Mark got it from Curly's friend when he jumped him to rescue M&M.

Chapter 2

1. Where was Bryon's mother, and why?
   She was in the hospital recovering from a serious operation.

2. How did Bryon describe himself and Mark?
   Bryon was the hustler and Mark was the thief.

3. Who was Randy? What did he do for the boys?
   Randy was a hippie college student who drove a Volkswagen bus. He picked the boys up when they were hitching a ride to the hospital. He also told them about the house where he lived.

4. Whom did Bryon's mother ask him to visit? What did Bryon learn about this person?
   She asked him to visit a boy in the hospital across the hall from her room. His name was Mike Chambers. He was in the hospital because he had been beaten up. He had stopped to help a black girl who was being harassed by a group of white boys. He drove her home. When he got to her house, a group of black boys surrounded the car. They asked her what they should do with him, and she said to kill him. The black boys beat him up, and he was in the hospital recovering. Mike said his father told him he was dumb.

5. Bryon said he had never been able to accept something. What was it?
   He had never been able to accept authority.

6. Describe Bryon's first meeting with Cathy.
   Bryon had gone to the hospital to visit his mother. He went to the snack bar. Cathy was working there, and recognized him, although he did not recognize her at first. Then he told her he wanted to talk to her sometime, and she agreed.

7. What was Mark's opinion of Mike? Who else had this opinion of Mike?
   Mark thought Mike was stupid, and so did Mike's father.

Chapter 3
1. Charlie said Bryon was honest in most ways, except one. In what area was Bryon dishonest? What was Bryon's answer to Charlie's comment?
   Charlie said Bryon lied like a dog. He said that was why Bryon could not get a job. Bryon was too mad to think about it, but promised himself he would think about it later. Then he asked Charlie if he could borrow his car on Saturday night, and Charlie agreed.

2. How did Bryon feel about Curtis, and why? What did Mark say the reason was?
    He couldn't stand Curtis. He said Curtis was conceited. Mark said it was because Angela dumped Bryon to make a play for Curtis, although he was not interested in her.

3. How did M&M's father treat him? What was Cathy's opinion of this treatment?
    M&M's father criticized him about his hair and his grades. Cathy thought her father should be praising him for his good grades, like English, and be happy he had never been in trouble.

4. What did Cathy say about Mark at the dance? What was Bryon's reaction?
    Cathy said Mark was beautiful, that she knew girls who would give their eyeteeth to have hair his color. Bryon felt hot and cold and sick and mad, all at once, for a second.

5. Describe the incident involving Mark. What happened, and why? What did Bryon do?
    Mark was trying to protect Curtis from a boy who was attacking Curtis. The attacker turned on Mark and hit him over the head with a bottle. By the time Bryon got to the scene, the police were there and had the boy in handcuffs. Bryon told the boy he would kill him. Then Bryon saw Angela talking to the boy and surmised that she had asked the boy to attack Curtis to get even with him because he was not interested in her. He changed his mind, and decided to get even with her instead of the boy. Then he asked Curtis if he knew Angela, and Curtis said no. Then Bryon went to the hospital with Mark.

6. How did the date with Cathy end?
    Curtis hot-wired Charlie's car and drove Cathy to the hospital. Bryon put Mark in the back seat, then dropped Cathy off. He didn't kiss her, because the porch light was on, and her little brothers and sisters were looking out the window. He said he would call her.

Chapters 4-5
1. How did Bryon and Mark spend the afternoon?
    They reminisced about the things they did when they were little kids. Then they talked about the way things were changing. Mark wondered why there was a difference, and Bryon said it was because, "that was then ,and this is now."

2. How did people at school feel about the fight?
    They were all mad at Angela, sympathized with Curtis, and thought a lot of Mark for stepping in to help Curtis.

3. Describe Bryon's mood on Monday.
    He was in a funny mood. He felt like he was standing apart from the others and watching. He felt like he could see through them. It was weird.

4. Describe the incident with the principal's car.
>Mark got caught bringing the principal's car back into its parking space at the school. Mark had been borrowing the car every week to drive down to see his probation officer on his lunch hour. The principal was laughing by the time Mark got through describing what he was doing, and why. The result was that the probation officer began picking Mark up at school each week.

5. What was Bryon's main problem about Cathy?
>She liked him, but he wanted her to be crazy about him.

6. Mark and Bryon hustled two men in the bar. What happened after they left the bar? Include all details, in order.
>The two Texans left the bar first. They stepped out of the alley next to the bar as the boys came out. Dirty Dave told them to step into the alley, and that he had a gun. The other one took the gun while Dirty Dave put on some brass knuckles. Mark told them they would know if they tackled with him. He used a voice that Bryon didn't recognize. Just then Charlie stepped into the alley and told them to put the gun down, because he was carrying a sawed-off shotgun. The Texans put the gun down and the boys walked past. Then one of the Texans reached for the gun and fired at them. Charlie slammed them to the ground. Mark grabbed the gun Charlie had dropped, and fired back at the Texans as they climbed over the wall. Bryon told Charlie he could get off of him, and the boys realized that Charlie had been shot above the eye, and was dead.

7. True or False: Bryon bought Charlie's car.
>False. The police gave it to him.

8. Who understood how Bryon felt, Cathy or Mark?
>Cathy understood, but Mark didn't.

9. Bryon said Mark was acting strange. What was he doing?
>He would stare at Bryon for long periods of time. It seemed to Bryon that Mark was trying to figure out who he (Bryon) was. Sometimes he acted jealous of Cathy.

Chapter 6

1. What happened to the Texans?
>They were sentenced to life in prison.

2. How did Bryon feel about the sentence the Texans got?
>He didn't feel glad, or vengeful, or anything. He didn't really care whether or not they got caught, because it would not bring Charlie back.

3. Cathy said there were problems at home with M&M. What were they?
   M&M was getting a lot of grief from his father for his hair and ideas. Cathy said he was going other places instead of staying home. She was afraid M&M would take drugs if he trusted the person who offered them.

4. How did Bryon say he felt about Cathy?
   He said he loved her, even though he thought it was corny.

5. What was The Ribbon, and what did Cathy, Mark, and Bryon do there?
   It was a two lane, two mile long stretch of roadway with hot dog and hamburger stands, drive-ins, and supermarkets along it. The kids all drove up and down socializing with other kids. One guy in a Corvette made an obscene remark. Mark got out of the car, punched the guy in the nose, and got back in the car. Then Bryon took off. They didn't see the Corvette again.

6. What did M&M do while they were at The Ribbon?
   He asked them to drive by the hot dog stand again, and when they did, he got out of the car. They asked when they should pick him up, and he replied that he was never going home. He walked off towards a group of boys sitting on a station wagon. When they went back a while later to get him, he was gone.

Chapter 7

1. What was Mr. Carlson's reaction to the news about his son? What did Cathy think?
   Mr. Carlson said M&M would be home the next day, that it was just a stage he was going through. Cathy said it was not just a stage, that it was important to acknowledge what he was feeling. She told her father it would be his fault if M&M never came home.

2. Where did Bryon get a job? What did he change to keep it?
   He got a job at a supermarket. He changed his attitude. Inwardly, he still thought smart-aleck things, but he did not say them.

3. Describe Mark and Bryon's meeting with Angela. Retell the events in order. Tell why the incident happened.
   Bryon and Mark went riding around at the Ribbon, and saw Angela. Mark suggested they pull in and talk to her. She got in the car with them and they rode around while she told them her problems. Then Mark found someone to buy liquor for them. Angela started drinking, and after a while she passed out. Bryon was also drinking. Mark stopped the car and cut off all of Angela's long, black hair. Then they took her home and dropped her and her hair in her front yard. The boys finished the rum, and Bryon cried on the way home.

4. Bryon said he knew why everyone wanted to be Mark's friend. What was the reason?
   Bryon thought everyone dreamed of having a pet lion to stand between them and the world. He thought of Mark as the lion. Nothing bad ever happened to him, because he didn't care about anything or anyone (except Bryon.)

5. How did Bryon find where M&M was?
   Mark said he knew, and would take Bryon the next day.

6. Retell the story Mark told about his parents.
   Mark was hiding under the porch and heard his parents arguing. Mark's father said no one in his family or in his mother's family had eyes the color of Mark's. The mother said Mark was not the father's son. They started yelling and he heard a sound like firecrackers. Then he thought he would go and live with Bryon and his mother.

7. Bryon told Mark he couldn't help something. What was it?
   He couldn't help thinking about things.

<u>Chapters 8-9</u>

1. Where did Bryon and Mark go to look for M&M? Did they find him?
   They went to an old part of town, to a large old house. Several of the people in the house knew Mark, and called him "Cat". One guy said M&M had been around, but was not there that day. He also said M&M was flying, and was going to crash.

2. What did Bryon and Mark discuss when they left the place?
   The talked about grass and rum. Mark said Bryon should not knock something because it was not his thing. Bryon said they were different because grass was illegal. Mark replied that the law was not necessarily right. Bryon did not understand why Mark was defending pot. Mark said he did not smoke it, but he did not like to hear Bryon judging people.

3. What happened to Bryon while he was waiting on the steps at Terry Jones's house?
   Tim and Curly Shephard and two other boys beat him up for cutting Angela's hair. Mark and Terry found him there later.

4. Did Bryon want to get even?
   No, he did not.

5. How did Mark feel about what happened to Bryon?
   Mark was very upset. He didn't know why Bryon would not let him get the Shepherds, especially since Bryon had taken the punishment for Mark's deed.

6. Mark said he had never worried about something before. What was it?
   He had never worried before about 'what if?'

7. Did Bryon and Mark understand each other's opinions?
   No, they did not.

8. Where did Bryon go, alone, when he got better? What did he do there?
   He drove out to the cemetery where Charlie was buried. He thanked Charlie for saving his life and letting him use the car.

9. Where did Bryon and Cathy go? What did they find? What did they do about it?
   The went back to the commune and found M&M. He was on a bad trip from LSD. They called Mr. Carlson, then took M&M to the hospital. Mr. Carlson met them there.

Chapters 10-11
1. What did Mr. Carlson tell Bryon? How did Bryon feel about it?
   Mr. Carlson said he appreciated what Bryon had done, and that he was proud of him. Bryon said it was the first time any man had called him 'son' without getting him mad.

2. Bryon said something was getting easier. What was it?
   Telling Cathy he loved her was getting easier.

3. What did Bryon find when he looked for Mark's cigarettes? What did he do after he found the item?
   He looked under Mark's mattress. He found a cylinder of pills. He realized Mark was selling drugs. He called the police and reported Mark.

4. What did Bryon tell Mark when he got home? What was Mark's reaction?
   Bryon told Mark he had called the police. Mark reminded Bryon what it could do to him, since he already had a record. When the police came, he stood quivering as Bryon told the police all he knew.

5. What did Bryon's mother say when she heard what had happened?
   His mother said she loved Mark, but Bryon was her son and he came first. She thought maybe the juvenile authorities could help Mark. She said what Mark had done was wrong, and Bryon told on him for his own good.

6. What punishment did Mark receive? Why did the judge give him that punishment?
   He got five years in the state reformatory. Bryon thought the judge went hard on him because of his attitude.

7. What happened to M&M?
   He cut his hair, and his old expression of trust and intent interest was gone. He said he didn't think he would ever have any children, because of possible chromosome damage. He also said his memory was gone, and his grades were poor.

8. What happened to Bryon and Cathy?
   Bryon stopped calling her. She began dating Ponyboy Curtis.

9. Describe the last meeting between Bryon and Mark.
   Bryon went to the reformatory. He tried to apologize. Mark said when he got out he was leaving and Bryon would never see him again. Bryon reminded him that they had been like brothers. Mark reminded Bryon that he had once said, "That was then, and this is now."

10. How did Bryon feel at the end of the story?
    He was too mixed up to care. He wished he could be a kid again, when he had all of the answers.

MULTIPLE CHOICE STUDY/QUIZ QUESTIONS *That Was Then*

<u>Chapter 1</u>

1. What was Bryon's problem at the bar? How did he solve it?
    A. He was too young to get a beer. He used a stolen identification card as proof of age to get served.
    B. Another drunk customer challenged him to a fight, and he didn't want to fight. He went into the bathroom and climbed out the window.
    C. He had three dollars of unpaid charges at the bar, and the bartender would not give him credit for a Coke. Mark promised to pay the next day.
    D. He was supposed to work as a dishwasher that night, but wanted to take time off to go on a date. He had his girlfriend pretend to be his mother, and call in sick for him.

2. True or False: Mark lived with Bryon and his mother.
    A. True
    B. False

3. How did Bryon describe the relationship between himself and Mark?
    A. They were casual acquaintances.
    B. They used to be friends, but weren't any more.
    C. They were good friends.
    D. They were like brothers.

4. Which of the following does **not** describe M&M?
    A. He was very serious, with a wide-eyed, trusting look on his face.
    B. He wore an old army jacket, moccasins, and a peace symbol around his neck.
    C. He was eleven years old.
    D. He had grey eyes and long, charcoal colored hair.

5. What 'talent' did Mark have, and what happened to him because of it?
    A. He could pick any lock. He had broken into a store and had gone to a reform school for a year.
    B. He could read upside down. He was able to look at papers on teachers' desks, and read test answers from other students' papers. So far he had not been caught, but his ability helped him get good grades.
    C. He could imitate voices. He made a lot of prank phone calls. The phone company traced the calls and threatened to disconnect his service if he did not stop it.
    D. He could hot-wire anything, and had been caught stealing a car. Now he was on probation, and had to see the probation officer weekly.

Multiple Choice Questions *That Was Then*

6. True or False: Curly had a grudge against Bryon because Bryon got the girl Curly wanted.
   A. True
   B. False

7. Bryon and Mark saved someone from being jumped, and now they were going to do the same thing to someone else. This person said their attitude made them sick. Who was it?
   A. It was Bryon's mother.
   B. It was M&M.
   C. It was Curtis.
   D. It was Douglas.

8. Where did Mark and Bryon get the money to pay Charlie?
   A. M&M loaned it to them.
   B. They broke into a few newspaper boxes.
   C. Bryon took it from his mother's wallet.
   D. Mark got it from Curly's friend when he jumped him.

Multiple Choice Questions *That Was Then*

Chapter 2

1. Where was Bryon's mother, and why?
    A. She was a career military officer, and was away at a training school.
    B. She was in a mental institution. She had a breakdown when her husband left her.
    C. She was working late on a big project.
    D. She was in the hospital recovering from a serious operation.

2. What transportation did Bryon and Mark use to visit her?
    A. They hitched a ride with a hippie in a Volkswagen bus.
    B. They walked.
    C. They stole a car and drove themselves.
    D. They hid on a train and got a free ride.

3. What happened while Bryon was visiting his mother?
    A. He met his mother's boss.
    B. He met Cathy.
    C. He got offered a part-time job.
    D. He was attacked by a security dog and had to get stitches and a rabies shot.

4. What did Bryon learn about Mike Chambers?
    A. A group of black boys beat him up after he helped a black girl.
    B. He had been in jail for hitting someone over the head with a bottle.
    C. He lived in a commune and studied English at the local college.
    D. He wanted to marry Bryon's mother.

5. What did Mark think about Mike Chambers?
    A. He thought Mike was very brave.
    B. He thought Mike was insane.
    C. He thought Mike was stupid.
    D. He thought Mike was a liar.

Multiple Choice Questions *That Was Then*

Chapter 3

1. Charlie said Bryon was honest in most ways, except one. In what area was Bryon dishonest?
    A. Bryon stole things.
    B. Bryon cheated in school.
    C. Bryon lied a lot.
    D. Bryon mistreated his girlfriends.

2. How did Bryon feel about Curtis, and why?
    A. He couldn't stand Curtis. He said Curtis was conceited.
    B. He liked Curtis and wanted to be friends.
    C. He was jealous because Curtis had a lot of money.
    D. He made fun of Curtis because he didn't like to fight.

3. True or False: Mark said Bryon didn't like Curtis because Angela dumped Bryon to make a play for Curtis.
    A. True
    B. False

4. Who criticized M&M about his hair and his grades?
    A. His teachers did.
    B. Cathy did.
    C. His friends, including Bryon and Mark, did.
    D. His father did.

5. What made Bryon feel hot and cold and sick and mad, all at once, for a second?
    A. Mark made a pass at Cathy.
    B. Cathy said Mark was beautiful.
    C. Cathy told Bryon he was not good enough for her.
    D. Angela told Cathy that Bryon was not a good choice for a boyfriend.

6. What happened to Mark, and why?
    A. He got caught trying to steal liquor from a car in the school parking lot. The owner of the car beat him up.
    B. He was not properly dressed for the dance and was not allowed in.
    C. A cute girl asked him to dance. She picked his pocket while they were dancing, then left him. Later he learned that Curly had set him up.
    D. Mark was trying to protect Curtis from a boy who was attacking him. The attacker turned on Mark and hit him over the head with a bottle.

Multiple Choice Questions *That Was Then*

7. True or False: Curtis hot-wired Charlie's car and drove Cathy to the hospital.
    A. True
    B. False

Multiple Choice Questions *That Was Then*

Chapters 4-5

1. How did Bryon and Mark spend the afternoon?
    A. Bryon took Mark to the doctor's office for an examination.
    B. They reminisced and talked about the way things were changing.
    C. They hung out at Charlie's.
    D. They drove around looking for Curly and Angela.

2. True or False: The kids at school blamed the fight on Mark.
    A. True
    B. False

3. Describe Bryon's mood on the Monday after the dance.
    A. He was the happiest he had been in a long time. He felt like the future held good things for him.
    B. He could hardly concentrate on his school work. He thought about suicide.
    C. He was very angry. He felt like smashing things and beating people up.
    D. He was in a funny mood. He felt like he was standing apart from the others and watching. He felt like he could see through them. It was weird.

4. What happened to Mark after he got caught driving the principal's car?
    A. Mark was sent to the special high school for students with discipline problems.
    B. The probation officer began picking Mark up at school each week.
    C. He was placed on in-school suspension for the rest of the year.
    D. He had to work for the principal every day to pay for gas and mileage for the car.

5. True or False: Cathy liked Bryon, but he wanted her to be crazy about him.
    A. True
    B. False

6. List the following events in order. They occur after Mark and Bryon left the bar.
    A. The two Texans told Mark and Bryon to step into the alley.
    B. One of the Texans fired a gun at Charlie, Bryon, and Mark.
    C. Mark fired a gun at the Texans.
    D. Mark told them they would know if they tackled with him.

Multiple Choice Questions *That Was Then*

7. What happened to Charlie?
    A. He was killed.
    B. He was wounded in the leg. The injury got him out of the draft.
    C. Nothing. Mark saved his life.
    D. He was arrested for possessing an illegal weapon.

8. True or False: Bryon and Mark bought Charlie's car.
    A. True
    B. False

9. True or False: Cathy understood, but Mark didn't.
    A. True
    B. False

10. Bryon said Mark was acting strange. What was he doing?
    A. He was laughing hysterically at everything.
    B. He was very angry. He would shout and throw things.
    C. He would stare at Bryon for long periods of time.
    D. He stopped eating and sleeping.

Multiple Choice Questions *That Was Then*

Chapter 6

1. What happened to the Texans?
    - A. They escaped.
    - B. The one who pulled the trigger got ten years. The other one got five years.
    - C. They were sentenced to life in prison.
    - D. There was a hung jury, so they got off.

2. True or False: Bryon didn't really care whether or not the Texans got caught.
    - A. True
    - B. False

3. Cathy said there were problems at home with M&M. Which of these was **not** one of them?
    - A. He was getting a lot of grief from his father for his hair and ideas.
    - B. He was beating up his little brothers and sisters.
    - C. He was going other places instead of staying home.
    - D. Cathy was afraid he would take drugs if he trusted the person who offered them.

4. True or False: Bryon was getting bored with Cathy and wanted to date someone more exciting.
    - A. True
    - B. False

5. The narrator described a two lane, two mile long stretch of roadway with hot dog and hamburger stands, drive-ins, and supermarkets along it. What was it called?
    - A. It was called the Snake.
    - B. It was called the Strip.
    - C. It was called the Dragway.
    - D. It was called the Ribbon.

Multiple Choice Questions *That Was Then*

6. What happened with the kids in the Corvette?
    A. One guy in a Corvette made an obscene remark. Mark got out of the car, punched the guy in the nose, and got back in the car. Then Bryon took off. They didn't see the Corvette again.
    B. They were racing Bryon and came up to a curve. They took it too fast and flipped the car. Both of them were injured.
    C. They deliberately bumped into the back of Bryon's car to irritate him. A police officer saw it, and arrested them.
    D. They were in line in front of Bryon at the drive-up window. They ordered a lot of food and then drove off without paying. The clerk thought Bryon and Mark had ordered it, and tried to charge them. Bryon and Mark chased the Corvette and made them come back and pay.

7. What did M&M do while they were out driving around?
    A. He got drunk.
    B. He asked them to let him out of the car, and said he was never going home again.
    C. He picked up a girl.
    D. He hid on the floor of the back seat because he didn't like what they were doing.

Multiple Choice Questions *That Was Then*

Chapter 7

1. True or False: Mr. Carlson called the police immediately and reported M&M as a runaway.
    A. True
    B. False

2. What did Bryon do to get and keep a job?
    A. He cut his hair and shaved.
    B. He begged Charlie for a reference.
    C. He lied about his age on the application.
    D. He stopped saying smart-aleck things, even though he still thought them.

3. Mark and Bryon met with Angela. List the events in order.
    A. They took her home and dropped her and her hair in her front yard.
    B. She got in the car with them and they rode around while she told them her problems.
    C. Mark stopped the car and cut off all of Angela's long, black hair.
    D. Angela started drinking, and after a while she passed out.

4. Bryon said he knew why everyone wanted to be Mark's friend. What image did he use to describe Mark?
    A. It was a pet lion.
    B. It was a guardian angel.
    C. It was a fierce guard dog.
    D. It was Sir Galahad.

5. How did Bryon find out where M&M was?
    A. He saw M&M one day and followed him.
    B. M&M called him and told him.
    C. Mark said he knew, and would take Bryon the next day.
    D. He found Randy at the college and asked him.

6. What happened to Mark's parents?
    A. They were both serving life terms in prison.
    B. They had left the country and could not return.
    C. His father was dead and his mother was in a mental institution.
    D. They shot and killed each other.

Multiple Choice Questions *That Was Then*

7. Bryon told Mark he couldn't help something. What was it?
    A. He couldn't help falling in love with Cathy.
    B. He couldn't help missing Charlie.
    C. He couldn't help thinking about things.
    D. He couldn't help worrying about his mother and his future.

Multiple Choice Questions *That Was Then*

Chapters 8-9

1. Where did Bryon and Mark go to look for M&M?
    A. They went to an old part of town , to a large old house that was being used as a commune.
    B. They went to a sit-in at the park.
    C. They went to Charlie's bar.
    D. They went to the recreation center at the college.

2. What did Bryon and Mark discuss when they left the place?
    A. They talked about war and peace.
    B. They wondered what it would be like to be hippies.
    C. The talked about the difference between using grass and rum.
    D. They talked about their own futures.

3. What happened to Bryon while he was waiting on the steps at Terry Jones's house?
    A. He was wounded in a drive-by shooting.
    B. Tim and Curly Shephard and two other boys beat him up for cutting Angela's hair.
    C. He was picked by the police on suspicion of burglary. Terry's neighbor had reported him.
    D. The guys in the Corvette drove by and threw rocks at his car. They broke all of the windows.

4. Did Bryon want to get even?
    A. Yes, he did.
    B. No, he did not.

5. Mark said he had never worried about something before. What was it?
    A. He had never worried about his future.
    B. He had never worried about not having a real family.
    C. He had never worried about 'what if?'
    D. He had never worried about his health.

6. Did Bryon and Mark understand each other's opinions?
    A. Yes, they did.
    B. No, they did not.

Multiple Choice Questions *That Was Then*

7. Where did Bryon go when he got better? What did he do there?
    A. He went the cemetery where Charlie was buried. He thanked Charlie for saving his life.
    B. He went to see his mother in the hospital and told her everything that was going on with him.
    C. He went to the Army recruiting office and enlisted.
    D. He went to visit Cathy. He asked her to marry him.

8. Bryon and Cathy found M&M at the commune. What was the next thing they did?
    A. They got M&M some lunch.
    B. They took M&M to the hospital.
    C. They got a broom and killed all of the spiders in the room.
    D. They called Mr. Carlson.

Multiple Choice Questions *That Was Then*

Chapters 10-11

1. Mr. Carlson called Bryon a name. Bryon said it was the first time someone called him this without him getting mad. What did Mr. Carlson call Bryon?
    A. Mr. Carlson called him 'kid.'
    B. Mr. Carlson called him 'BD.'
    C. Mr. Carlson called him 'punk.'
    D. Mr. Carlson called him 'son.'

2. Bryon said something was getting easier. What was it?
    A. Telling Cathy he loved her was getting easier.
    B. Thinking like an adult was getting easier.
    C. Talking to his mother was getting easier.
    D. Doing things without Mark was getting easier.

3. What did Bryon find when he looked for Mark's cigarettes?
    A. He found an envelope full of money.
    B. He found ten gold watches.
    C. He found a cylinder of pills.
    D. He found a tin can full of marijuana.

4. What else did Bryon do just before Mark got home?
    A. He called the police and told them all he knew.
    B. He called Cathy and asked her what to do.
    C. He put Mark's clothes and other personal items in a bag and put it by the door.
    D. He sat on the bed and cried.

5. Who said the juvenile authorities might be able to help Mark?
    A. Cathy did.
    B. Mr. Carlson did.
    C. Bryon's mother did.
    D. Mark's probation officer did.

6. True or False: Mark was sentenced to five years in the state reformatory.
    A. True
    B. False

Multiple Choice Questions *That Was Then*

7. Which of the following did **not** happen to M&M?
    A. He cut his hair.
    B. His father kicked him out of the house permanently.
    C. His old expression of trust and intent interest was gone.
    D. His grades were poor.

8. True or False: Bryon stopped calling Cathy.
    A. True
    B. False

9. What did Mark tell Bryon he would do when he got out?
    A. Mark said he would get even with Bryon.
    B. Mark said he wanted things to go back to the way they were.
    C. Mark said he wanted to reform and live a clean life.
    D. Mark said when he got out he was leaving and Bryon would never see him again.

10. True or False: Bryon had everything figured out at the end of the story.
    A. True
    B. False

STUDENT ANSWER SHEET-MULTIPLE CHOICE/QUIZ QUESTIONS
That Was Then, This Is Now

Chapter 1
1. _____
2. _____
3. _____
4. _____
5. _____
6. _____
7. _____
8. _____
9. _____

Chapter 2
1. _____
2. _____
3. _____
4. _____
5. _____
6. _____

Chapter 3
1. _____
2. _____
3. _____
4. _____
5. _____
6. _____
7. _____

Chapters 4-5
1. _____
2. _____
3. _____
4. _____
5. _____
6. _____
7. _____
8. _____
9. _____
10 _____

Chapter 6
1. _____
2. _____
3. _____
4. _____
5. _____
6. _____
7. _____

Chapter 7
1. _____
2. _____
3. _____
4. _____
5. _____
6. _____
7. _____

Chapters 8-9
1. _____
2. _____
3. _____
4. _____
5. _____
6. _____
7. _____
8. _____
9. _____
10. _____

Chapters 10-11
1. _____
2. _____
3. _____
4. _____
5. _____
6. _____
7. _____
8. _____
9. _____
10. _____

ANSWER KEY-MULTIPLE CHOICE/QUIZ QUESTIONS
That Was Then, This Is Now

Chapter 1	Chapter 2	Chapter 3	Chapters 4-5
1. C	1. D	1. C	1. B
2. A True	2. A	2. A	2. B False
3. D	3. B	3. A True	3. D
4. C	4. A	4. D	4. B
5. D	5. C	5. B	5. A True
6. B False		6. D	6. A D B C
7. B		7. A True	7. A
8. D			8. B False
			9. A True
			10. C

Chapter 6	Chapter 7	Chapters 8-9	Chapters 10-11
1. C	1. B False	1. A	1. D
2. A True	2. D	2. C	2. A
3. B	3. B D C A	3. B	3. C
4. B False	4. A	4. B	4. A
5. D	5. C	5. C	5. C
6. A	6. D	6. B	6. A True
7. B	7. C	7. A	7. B
		8. D	8. A True
			9. D
			10. B False

PREREADING VOCABULARY WORKSHEETS

Vocabulary Worksheets *That Was Then, This Is Now*

Chapter 1
Part I: Using Prior Knowledge and Context Clues
Below are the sentences in which the vocabulary words appear in the text. Read each sentence. Use any clues you can find in the sentence combined with your prior knowledge, and write what you think the underlined words mean on the lines provided.

1. Mark and me went down to the bar/pool hall about two or three blocks from where we lived with the ***sole*** intention of making some money.
   _____

2. "You're right," Mark said. "But I really sounded ***profound*** there for a minute, huh?"
   _____

3. "Let's go look for M&M," Mark said ***abruptly*** and we left.
   _____

4. "My sister's home," he added as an afterthought. "No kidding?" asked Mark ***tactfully***, thumbing through a *Playboy*. "Which one?"
   _____

5. "Yeah, well, you're on ***probation*** now for 'borrowing,' so I don't think it's such a great idea," I said.
   _____

6. "Hey, flower child, turn around," they were ***taunting*** him, but M&M just kept right on moving.
   _____

Part II: Determining the Meaning Match the vocabulary words to their dictionary definitions.

_____ 1. sole   A. suddenly
_____ 2. profound   B. supervised freedom for lawbreakers
_____ 3. abruptly   C. insulting
_____ 4. tactfully   D. single; only
_____ 5. probation   E. dealing with people in a skillful way
_____ 6. taunting   F. intellectual

Vocabulary Worksheets *That Was Then, This Is Now*

Chapter 2
Part I: Using Prior Knowledge and Context Clues
Below are the sentences in which the vocabulary words appear in the text. Read each sentence. Use any clues you can find in the sentence combined with your prior knowledge, and write what you think the underlined words mean on the lines provided.

1. As a result, I was putting on weight--I wasn't in much danger of getting fat since it seemed like I was growing an inch taller a week--and Mark was staying as ***slight*** and slender as ever. You'd never guess Mark was as strong as he was by looking at him, but I knew. . . he was as tough as a piece of leather.
   _____

2. If there was a ***lame*** dog within three miles, she'd find it.
   _____

3. I was five-ten at sixteen and still growing, but I went through my ***lanky*** period at fourteen and I had a good build, of which I was proud.
   _____

4. "The last time that happened, my brother busted a bottle over the guy's head and got charged with ***assault*** with a dangerous weapon."
   _____

5. As we got into the elevator, Mark said, "I'm ***inclined*** to agree with his old man. That is one stupid guy."
   _____

Part II: Determining the Meaning Match the vocabulary words to their dictionary definitions.

   _____ 1. slight   A. attack
   _____ 2. lame   B. tall and skinny
   _____ 3. lanky   C. light in form or build
   _____ 4. assault   D. likely or tending to
   _____ 5. inclined   E. having an injured foot or leg

Vocabulary Worksheets *That Was Then, This Is Now*

Chapter 3

Part I: Using Prior Knowledge and Context Clues
Below are the sentences in which the vocabulary words appear in the text. Read each sentence. Use any clues you can find in the sentence combined with your prior knowledge, and write what you think the underlined words mean on the lines provided.

1. "For one thing, you know how often the plainclothes cops stop in. Do you think they'd let a ***minor*** work here? You're lucky you can just come in and sit down."
   _____

2. She was smiling with that ***sassy*** smirk, and I wondered why on earth I'd ever given a damn about her.
   _____

3. Her face was ***contorted*** for a second, and she called me a few names and flounced off.
   _____

4. Her face was contorted for a second, and she called me a few names and ***flounced*** off.
   _____

5. "Then the cops showed up. Right in the nick of time," he added ***sarcastically***.
   _____

Part II: Determining the Meaning   Match the vocabulary words to their dictionary definitions.

____ 1.	minor	A.	twisted out of shape
____ 2.	sassy	B.	one who is below the legal age
____ 3.	contorted	C.	rude
____ 4.	flounced	D.	in a mocking manner
____ 5.	sarcastically	E.	moved in a bouncy or lively manner

Vocabulary Worksheets *That Was Then, This Is Now*

Chapters 4-5
Part I: Using Prior Knowledge and Context Clues
Below are the sentences in which the vocabulary words appear in the text. Read each sentence. Use any clues you can find in the sentence combined with your prior knowledge, and write what you think the underlined words mean on the lines provided.

1. But Mark was always the ***hub*** of this circle of people, and I was always with Mark.
   _____

2. "We've had some good times, huh, Bryon?" Mark broke the silence. I guess we both had been ***reminiscing***.
   _____

3. This can make for problems. It used to, anyway, with the Socs beating up the greasers, but in these days, with all that love, peace, and groove stuff, the fights had ***slacked*** off.
   _____

4. I have a ***vague*** notion that the Left is Hippie and the Right is Hick, but I really don't know much else.
   _____

5. "I happened to be standing around when the ***aforementioned*** incident occurred."
   _____

6. This was an invitation for me to buy her a soda, so I said ***obligingly,*** "Want a Coke?"
   _____

7. "See ya 'round, kids," the Texans said as they ***sauntered*** out.
   _____

8. We couldn't resist ***smirking*** a little as we walked past the Texans. Even in the dark I could see the anger contorting their faces.
   _____

Vocabulary Worksheets *That Was Then, This Is Now*

Part II: Determining the Meaning Match the vocabulary words to their dictionary definitions.

_____	1. hub	A.	sneering
_____	2. reminiscing	B.	willingly
_____	3. slacked	C.	indistinct
_____	4. vague	D.	strolled
_____	5. aforementioned	E.	slowed
_____	6. obligingly	F.	center
_____	7. sauntered	G.	said before
_____	8. smirking	H.	remembering past events

Vocabulary Worksheets *That Was Then, This Is Now*

Chapters 6-7

Part I: Using Prior Knowledge and Context Clues

Below are the sentences in which the vocabulary words appear in the text. Read each sentence. Use any clues you can find in the sentence combined with your prior knowledge, and write what you think the underlined words mean on the lines provided.

1. He watched me closely at first-- I guess he couldn't forget that by the time the police had showed up at Charlie's I had been ***hysterical.*** He didn't have to worry. I went through the whole trial calm, collected, numb, and empty.

   _____

2. I didn't feel glad, or ***vengeful,*** or anything. I really hadn't much cared whether or not they even caught those guys.

   _____

3. I was puzzled. "So what?" She gave me an ***incredulous*** look. "So what? Have you smoked it?"

   _____

4. Cathy was sitting next to me, Mark on her other side, and M&M was hanging out the window, ***gravely*** watching people, waving if he was waved to, yelling back if he was yelled at, always slightly surprised at the crudity of the calls, as if he hadn't heard the same things a hundred thousand times before.

   _____

5. I realized right then that whatever chance Mark and Cathy had of becoming friends was gone. I had already sensed in Cathy the same ***hostility*** toward mark that he had for her.

   _____

6. "Then why didn't you ever tell him so?" Cathy sobbed ***irrationally.***

   _____

7. One night a couple of weeks after M&M disappeared, Mark and me went goofing around by ourselves again. It was almost as if we had never felt a ***gulf*** between us, never been separated by something we couldn't see.

   _____

Vocabulary Worksheets *That Was Then, This Is Now*

Part II: Determining the Meaning Match the vocabulary words to their dictionary definitions.

_____ 1. hysterical   A. in an uncontrolled, excitable state
_____ 2. vengeful   B. seriously
_____ 3. incredulous   C. distance
_____ 4. gravely   D. not logically
_____ 5. hostility   E. doubtful
_____ 6. irrationally   F. ill will; extreme anger
_____ 7. gulf   G. wanting to give punishment for a wrong

Vocabulary Worksheets *That Was Then, This Is Now*

Chapters 8-9

Part I: Using Prior Knowledge and Context Clues
Below are the sentences in which the vocabulary words appear in the text. Read each sentence. Use any clues you can find in the sentence combined with your prior knowledge, and write what you think the underlined words mean on the lines provided.

1. "Brother, you look like you been through a meat grinder." "That's what it feels like, too," I said, even though this **witticism** cost me more stabbing pains in my sides.
   _____

2. Mom nearly had a fit when she saw me. She was well by then, back at her job. I almost gave her a **relapse**. I had never been so messed up.
   _____

3. "Yeah. Mark says he's seen him at this hippie **commune**-house." Cathy looked shocked. "One of those free-love places?"
   _____

Part II: Determining the Meaning Match the vocabulary words to their dictionary definitions.

____ 1. witticism   A. a group of people living together
____ 2. relapse   B. slipping back
____ 3. commune   C. joke

Vocabulary Worksheets *That Was Then, This Is Now*

Chapters 10-11
Part I: Using Prior Knowledge and Context Clues
Below are the sentences in which the vocabulary words appear in the text. Read the sentence. Use any clues you can find in the sentence combined with your prior knowledge, and write what you think the underlined words mean on the lines provided.

1. "Bryon, you know what something like this would do to me with my record. Bryon, tell me you're lyin'." Mark was ***pleading*** desperately.

2. "Bryon, you know what something like this would do to me with my record. Bryon, tell me you're lyin'." Mark was pleading ***desperately.***

3. Mark had a hearing, or a trial, or whatever--I never paid any attention to the ***formalities.***

4. "O.K.," he said, but he looked half-scared, and his old expression of complete trust and ***intent*** interest was gone entirely. He looked like a little kid--I had forgotten he was just a little kid.

5. I seemed to have become a mixture of things I had picked up from Charlie, Mark, Cathy, M&M, Mom, and even ***obscure*** people like Mike and the blonde hippie-chick and the Shephards.

Part II: Determining the Meaning Match the vocabulary words to their dictionary definitions.

_____ 1. pleading   A. customs
_____ 2. desperately   B. begging
_____ 3. formalities   C. unclear
_____ 4. intent   D. hopelessly
_____ 5. obscure   E. resolute

ANSWER SHEET PREREADING VOCABULARY
That Was Then, This Is Now

Directions: Fill in the correct chapter number. Use as many of the lines as needed for each chapter.

Chapter____   Chapter____

Part 1   Pt.2   Part 1   Pt.2
1._____ _____   1._____ _____
2._____ _____   2._____ _____
3._____ _____   3._____ _____
4._____ _____   4._____ _____
5._____ _____   5._____ _____
6._____ _____   6._____ _____
7._____ _____   7._____ _____
8._____ _____   8._____ _____
9._____ _____   9._____ _____
10._____ _____   10._____ _____

Chapter____   Chapter____

Part 1   Pt.2   Part 1   Pt.2
1._____ _____   1._____ _____
2._____ _____   2._____ _____
3._____ _____   3._____ _____
4._____ _____   4._____ _____
5._____ _____   5._____ _____
6._____ _____   6._____ _____
7._____ _____   7._____ _____
8._____ _____   8._____ _____
9._____ _____   9._____ _____
10._____ _____   10._____ _____

ANSWER KEY-PREREADING VOCABULARY WORKSHEETS
That Was Then, This Is Now

Chapter 1

1. D
2. F
3. A
4. E
5. B
6. C

Chapter 2

1. C
2. E
3. B
4. A
5. D

Chapter 3

1. B
2. C
3. A
4. E
5. D

Chapters 4-5

1. F
2. H
3. E
4. C
5. G
6. B
7. D
8. A

Chapters 6-7

1. A
2. G
3. E
4. B
5. F
6. D
7. C

Chapters 8-9

1. C
2. B
3. A

Chapters 10-11

1. B
2. D
3. A
4. E
5. C

DAILY LESSONS

LESSON ONE

Student Objectives
    1. To preview the *That Was Then, This Is Now* Unit
    2. To receive books and other related materials (study guides, reading assignment)
    3. To relate prior knowledge to the new material
    4. To discuss the non-fiction assignment

Activity #1
    Show students the cover of the book. Ask them to describe the cover, and discuss what the title might mean.

Activity #2
    Distribute the materials students will use in this unit. Explain in detail how students are to use these materials.

    Study Guides Students should preview the study guide questions before each reading assignment to get a feeling for what events and ideas are important in that section. After reading the section, students will (as a class or individually) answer the questions to review the important events and ideas from that section of the book. Students should keep the study guides as study materials for the unit test.

    Reading Assignment Sheet You need to fill in the reading assignment sheet to let students know when their reading has to be completed. You can either write the assignment sheet on a side blackboard or bulletin board and leave it there for students to see each day, or you can duplicate copies for each student to have. In either case, you should advise students to become very familiar with the reading assignments so they know what is expected of them.

    Unit Outline You may find it helpful to distribute copies of the Unit Outline to your students so they can keep track of upcoming lessons and assignments. You may also want to post a copy of the Unit Outline on a bulletin board and cross off each lesson as you complete it.

    Extra Activities Center The Unit Resources portion of this unit contains suggestions for a library of related books and articles in your classroom as well as crossword and word search puzzles. Make an Extra Activities center in your room where you will keep these materials for students to use. Bring the books and articles in from the library and keep several copies of the puzzles on hand. Explain to students that these materials are available for students to use when they finish reading assignments or other class work early.

    Books Each school has its own rules and regulations regarding student use of school books. Advise students of the procedures that are normal for your school.

Notebook or Unit Folder You may want the students to keep all of their worksheets, notes, and other papers for the unit together in a binder or notebook. During the first class meeting, tell them how you want them to arrange the folder. Make divider pages for vocabulary worksheets, prereading study guide questions, review activities, notes, and tests. You may want to give a grade for accuracy in keeping the folder.

Activity #3

Do a group KWL Sheet with the students (form included.) Some students will know something about S. E. Hinton or her books and will have information to share. Put this information in the K column (What I Know.) Ask students what they want to find out from reading the book and record this in the W column (What I Want to Find Out.) Keep the sheet and refer back to it after reading the book. Complete the L column (What I Learned) at that time.

Activity #4

Distribute copies of the Nonfiction Assignment sheet and go over it in detail with the students. Explain to students that they each are to read at least one nonfiction piece at some time during the unit. This could be a book, a magazine article, or information from an encyclopedia or the Internet. Students will fill out a nonfiction assignment sheet after completing the reading to help you (the teacher) evaluate their reading experiences and to help the students think about and evaluate their own reading experiences. Give them the due date for the assignment (Lesson 19.)

Encourage students to read about topics that are related to the theme of the novel. Some suggestions are: teen-aged gangs, juvenile delinquency, life in low-income neighborhoods, the effects of trauma or stress on teen-agers, use of drugs and alcohol by teen-agers, parent-child relationships, drug and alcohol rehabilitation programs, the importance of the peer group, teen-agers in prisons or reformatories, and teen-aged depression.

KWL *That Was Then, This Is Now*

Directions: Before reading, think about what you already know about S. E. Hinton and/or *That Was Then, This Is Now.* Write the information in the K column. Think about what you would like to find out from reading the book. Write your questions in the W column. After you have read the book, use the L column to write the answers to your questions from the W column, and anything else you remember from the book.

K **What I Know**	**W** **What I Want to Find Out**	**L** **What I Learned**

NONFICTION ASSIGNMENT SHEET *That Was Then, This Is Now*
(To be completed after reading the required nonfiction article)

Name _____ Date _____ Class _____

Title of Nonfiction Read _____

Written By _____ Publication Date _____

I. Factual Summary: Write a short summary of the piece you read.

II. Vocabulary:
    1. Which vocabulary words were difficult?

    2. What did you do to help yourself understand the words?

III. Interpretation: What was the main point the author wanted you to get from reading his/her work?

IV. Criticism:
    1. Which points of the piece did you agree with or find easy to believe? Why?

    2. With which points of the piece did you disagree or find difficult to believe? Why?

V. Personal Response:
    1. What do you think about this piece?

    2. How does this piece help you better understand the novel *That Was Then, This Is Now?*

LESSON TWO

Student Objectives
    1. To complete the pre-reading vocabulary work for Chapter 1
    2. To preview the study questions for Chapter 1
    3. To read Chapter 1
    4. To understand plot development and record plot information on a chart

Activity #1
    Work through the prereading vocabulary worksheet for Chapter 1 with the students. Tell them they will have a sheet like this to complete before reading each section of the book.

Activity #2
    Show students how to preview the study questions for Chapter 1. Encourage students to predict what they think answers might be, to write down their predictions, and to compare these with their answers after reading the chapter.

Activity #3
    Read the first few pages of Chapter 1 aloud to the students. Then ask for volunteers to read the rest of the chapter aloud.

Activity #4 Minilesson: Plot Development
    Tell students they will be discussing and mapping the plot of the novel. **Plot** refers to the sequence of events and conflicts. It tells what the characters do, what happens to them, and how things happen. The plot is usually divided into three main parts. In the **introduction** or **beginning**, the author introduces the characters, establishes the setting, and introduces a problem. During the **development** or **complication**, events unfold and conflicts increase. These events and conflicts create the suspense that keeps the reader interested. The **climax** is the highest point of action or suspense. The reader does not yet know the outcome. The climax separates the middle and end of the story. The **resolution** or **outcome** occurs at the end of the story. The problem is usually solved.
    Distribute copies of the Plot Diagram. Complete the beginning of the Plot Diagram with students. They should be able to identify the two major characters (Bryon and Mark), identify one problem (they don't have enough money to pay their bill at the bar) and foreshadow another (Charlie tells them they are going to get into trouble with their pool hustling.)
    Students will add information to the plot diagram during Lessons 6 and 13.

PLOT DIAGRAM

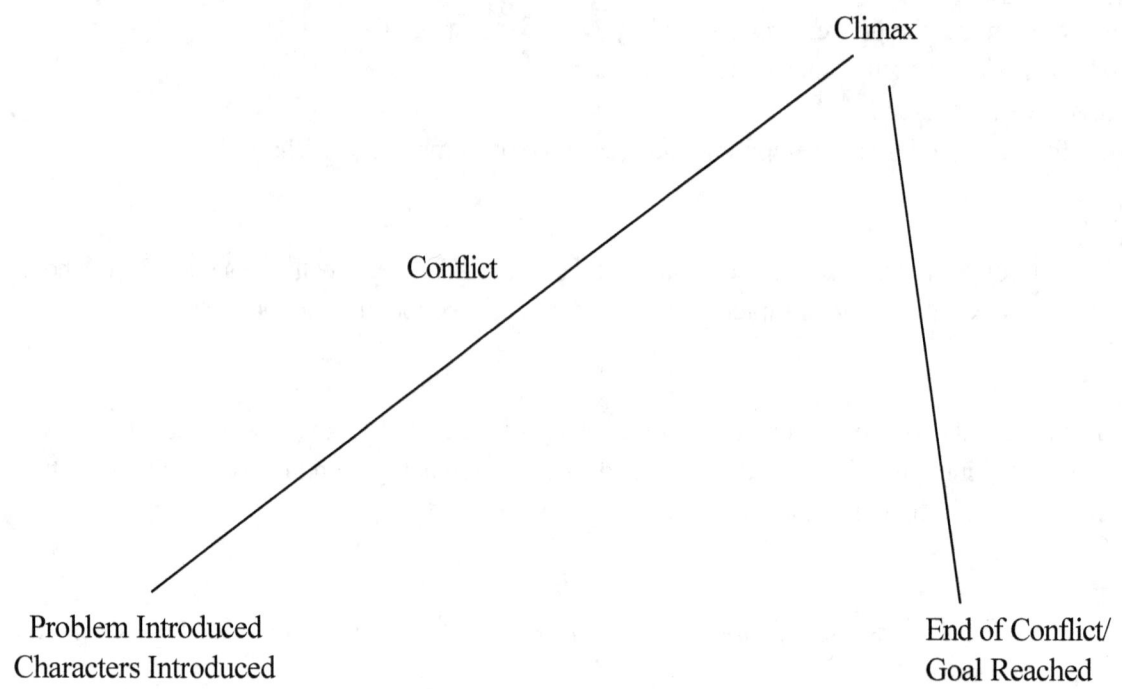

LESSON THREE

Student Objectives
    1. To discuss the main ideas and events in Chapter 1
    2. To identify the types of conflict in the novel
    3. To complete the prereading vocabulary work for Chapter 2
    4. To preview the study guide questions for Chapter 2
    5. To silently read Chapter 2

Activity #1

    Discuss the answers to the Study Guide questions for Chapter 1 in detail. Write the answers on the board or overhead projector so students can have the correct answers for study purposes. Encourage students to take notes. If the students own their books, encourage them to use high lighter pens to mark important passages and the answers to the study guide questions.

Activity #2 Minilesson: Conflict

    Tell students that conflict is one of the most important aspects of a work of fiction. The conflict usually is an obstacle to the main character's goal. It usually brings about some type of change in the main character. The different types of conflict are character vs. nature, character vs. character, character vs. society, and character vs. self (inner conflict.)

    You may want to use examples from stories the students have previously read, or examples from literature for younger children to illustrate the various types of conflict. Dorothy in *The Wizard of Oz* has a conflict with nature because the tornado takes her away from her home. The conflict between Cinderella and her wicked step-mother is an example of character vs. character. In *The Little Engine That Could*, the little engine is not sure of its ability to take the train over the mountain, illustrating the character vs. self conflict. The Greek myth of Atalanta illustrates character vs. society or the environment. Atalanta was expected to marry the man her father chose, but she did not wish to do so.

    Have students begin filling out the Conflict Chart after they have read Chapter 2. Discuss their findings. Encourage them to look for more examples of conflict as they read, and record them on the chart. Tell them they will discuss conflict again in Lesson Fourteen, during the Extra Discussion Questions.

Activity #3

    Give students about ten or fifteen minutes to do the prereading vocabulary work and preview the study questions for Chapter 2.

Activity #4

    Use the rest of the class period to silently read Chapter 2. Remind students that the reading should be completed before the next class meeting.

CONFLICT CHART
That Was Then, This Is Now

Type of Conflict	Story	Example of Conflict
CHARACTER VS. NATURE		
CHARACTER VS. SELF		
CHARACTER VS. SOCIETY		
CHARACTER VS. CHARACTER		

LESSON FOUR

Student Objectives
1. To discuss the main ideas and events in Chapter 2
2. To complete the prereading vocabulary work for Chapter 3
3. To preview the study questions for Chapter 3
4. To read Chapter 3 orally for evaluation

Activity #1

Divide the students into seven groups. Have each group prepare the answer to one study question and present it to the class.

Activity #2

Give students about ten minutes to complete the prereading vocabulary work and look over the study guide questions for Chapter 3.

Activity #3

Tell students their oral reading ability will be evaluated. Show them copies of the Oral Reading Evaluation Form and discuss it. Model correct intonation and expression by reading the first few paragraphs of Chapter 3 aloud.

Activity #4

Call on individual students to read a few paragraphs aloud as the other students follow silently in their books. If you have a student who is unwilling or unable to read in front of the group make arrangements to do his or her evaluation privately at another time.

Activity #5

Remind students to complete the answers to the study guide questions for the next class period.

LESSON FIVE

Student Objectives
1. To discuss the main ideas and events in Chapter 3
2. To begin Writing Assignment #1

Activity #1
Have students discuss the answers to the study guide questions with a partner. Then invite pairs to present their answers to the class.

Activity #2
Distribute copies of Writing Assignment #1. Go over the assignment in detail with the students. Tell them they will have the remainder of the class period to begin working on the assignment. Tell them it will be due at the next class meeting.

Activity #3
Distribute copies of the Writing Evaluation Form (included with this Unit Plan.) Explain to students that during Lesson Eight you will be holding individual writing conferences about this writing assignment. Make sure students are familiar with the criteria on the Writing Evaluation Form.

Follow-Up
After the individual writing conferences, allow students to revise their papers using your suggestions to complete the revisions. Grade the revisions on an A-C-E scale: A = all revisions well done; C = some revisions made; E = few or no revisions made. This will speed your grading time and still give some credit for the students' efforts.

ORAL READING EVALUATION *That Was Then, This Is Now*

Name_____ Class_____ Date _____

SKILL	Excellent	Good	Average	Fair	Poor
FLUENCY	5	4	3	2	1
CLARITY	5	4	3	2	1
AUDIBILITY	5	4	3	2	1
PRONUNCIATION	5	4	3	2	1
_____	5	4	3	2	1
_____	5	4	3	2	1

TOTAL _____ GRADE _____

COMMENTS:

WRITING ASSIGNMENT #1 *That Was Then*
Writing to Inform

PROMPT

You are a reporter for the high school newspaper. You overhear Bryon and Mark talking in the hall one day about some of their recent adventures, and decide to write a news article about one of them. For this assignment, choose any of the events that have occurred so far in your reading. Suggestions are: Bryon and Mark saving M&M from a beating, Chapter 1; the attack on Mike Chambers, Chapter 2; Mark's fight, Chapter 3.

PREWRITING

A news article must answer six basic questions: **Who** is the story about?; **What** happened?; **When** did it happen?; **Where** did it happen?; **Why** did it happen?; **How** did it happen? Before you interview one of the characters, make a list of the questions you want to ask him/her. Then reread the novel to find the answers to your questions. Once you have answered the 5W and H questions, decide on their order of importance for your article. Number them on your list. Make a list of these questions on a sheet of paper.

DRAFTING

Write a rough draft of your news article. Check your list to make sure you have included all of the information. Make sure you put the most important information from your list first in the story. Then create the headline. The headline tells the main idea of the story. It usually includes who is in the story and what happened. A headline does not have to be a complete sentence, but it should have a powerful verb. Read some headlines in your local newspaper to get the idea before you write yours. Next, put your byline and dateline on the news article. The byline is the name of the writer. It goes under the headline, on the right side of the page. The dateline is the date and place where the story took place. It goes on the first line of the story, before the story begins. Remember, a news article reports only the facts--don't put your personal opinion in the article.

PROMPT

When you finish the rough draft, ask another student to look at it. You may want to give the student your notes so he/she can double check for you and see that you have included all of the information. After reading, he or she should tell you what he/she liked best about your news article, which parts were difficult to understand or needed more information, and ways in which your work could be improved. Reread your news article considering your critic's comments and make the corrections you think are necessary.

PROOFREADING/EDITING

Do a final proofreading of your news article, double-checking your grammar, spelling, organization, and the clarity of your ideas.

WRITING EVALUATION FORM *That Was Then*

Name _____ Date _____ Class _____

Writing Assignment # ___

Circle One For Each Item:

Composition	excellent	good	fair	poor
Style	excellent	good	fair	poor
Grammar	excellent	good	fair	poor (errors noted)
Spelling	excellent	good	fair	poor (errors noted)
Punctuation	excellent	good	fair	poor (errors noted)
Legibility	excellent	good	fair	poor (errors noted)

Strengths:

Weaknesses:

Comments/Suggestions:

LESSON SIX

Student Objectives
1. To complete the prereading vocabulary work for Chapters 4-5
2. To preview the study questions for Chapters 4-5
3. To read Chapters 4-5
4. To add information to the plot diagram

Activity #1

Give students ten or fifteen minutes to complete the prereading vocabulary worksheet and read over the study questions.

Activity #2

Ask for volunteers to take the parts of the characters and read the chapters aloud to the class. Encourage students to dramatize their reading.

Activity #3

Have students work in small groups to discuss examples of conflict in Chapters 2-5. Then have a whole class discussion and decide which examples to add to the plot diagram. Remind students to continue adding to the plot diagram. It will be discussed again in Lesson Twelve.

LESSON SEVEN

Student Objectives
1. To discuss the main ideas and events in Chapters 4-5
2. To complete the prereading vocabulary work for Chapter 6
3. To preview the study questions for Chapter 6
4. To read Chapter 6 silently
5. To discuss the main ideas and events in Chapter 6

Activity #1

Invite students to dramatize the answers to the study questions for Chapters 4-5. .

Activity #2

Give students about fifteen minutes to complete the prereading vocabulary worksheet and preview the study questions for Chapter 6.

Activity #3

Tell students to read Chapter 6 silently and answer the study questions.

Activity #4

Go over the answers to the study questions for Chapter 6.

LESSON EIGHT

Student Objectives
    1. To demonstrate knowledge of the main ideas and events in the story so far
    2. To participate in a writing conference with the teacher
    3. To complete the prereading vocabulary work for Chapter 7
    4. To preview the study questions for Chapter 7
    5. To read Chapter 7 silently

Activity #1
    Hold individual writing conferences in a quiet corner of the room. Give them a due date for the revisions.

Activity #2
    Students may use the rest of the class time while you are conferencing to complete the prereading vocabulary worksheet, preview the study questions, read, and answer the study questions for Chapter 7. Tell them all work must be completed for the next class meeting.

LESSON NINE

Student Objectives
    1. To discuss the main ideas and events in Chapter 7
    2. To practice writing to persuade

Activity #1
    Have students discuss the answers to the study guide questions in small groups. Circulate among the groups and answer any questions.

Activity #2
    Ask students to think about a time someone tried to persuade them to do or not do something, or they tried to persuade someone. Invite pairs or small groups of students to role play such an occasion. Discuss the kinds of arguments they used, and their effectiveness. Tell them they will have the opportunity to persuade one of the characters in the story to do or not do something.

Activity #3
    Distribute copies of Writing Assignment #2. Give students the rest of the class period to work on it. Assign a due date if they do not finish in class.

WRITING ASSIGNMENT #2 *That Was Then*
Writing to Persuade

PROMPT

There are several occasions in Chapters 1-6 of *That Was Then, This Is Now* when one of the characters makes a choice you might disagree with. Skim through the chapters to find one of these occasions. Then pretend you are a friend, guidance counselor, or relative of the character, and persuade him or her to see your point of view. Some suggestions are: stop Bryon and Mark from hustling pool; stop Charlie from allowing minors in his bar, persuade Charlie to give you a job, persuade M&M to come home, persuade Mr. Carlson to stop picking on M&M.

PREWRITING

Make a list of the reasons you think the character should change. Think of statements to support each of your reasons, and list them under each reason. Then number the reasons in order from most to least important.

DRAFTING

Make an introductory statement in which you state what you want and why.

Use one paragraph for each of your reasons. Use the supporting statements for each reason. Summarize your talk by restating what you want.

PEER CONFERENCING/REVISING

When you finish the rough draft, ask another student to look at it. You may want to give the student your checklist so he/she can double check for you and see that you have included all of the information. After reading, he or she should tell you what he/she liked best about your persuasive talk, which parts were difficult to understand or needed more information, and ways in which your work could be improved. Reread your persuasive talk considering your critic's comments and make the corrections you think are necessary.

PROOFREADING/EDITING

Do a final proofreading of your persuasive talk, double-checking your grammar, spelling, organization, and the clarity of your ideas.

FINAL DRAFT

Follow your teacher's guidelines for completing the final draft of your persuasive talk.

LESSON TEN

Student Objectives
    1. To identify and interpret figurative language
    2. To complete the prereading vocabulary work for Chapters 8-9
    3. To preview the study questions for Chapters 8-9
    4. To read Chapters 8-9

Activity #1 Minilesson: Figures of Speech

    Figures of speech are literary devices that give the writer a non-literal way to describe images and events. Use the following chart to give examples of the different figures of speech. Then write "I look like a baby-faced kid" on the board. (Bryon uses this description of himself on page 1 of *That Was Then, This Is Now*.) Ask students to identify the type of figure of speech (simile.) Talk about the literal meaning. Distribute the Figure of Speech worksheet and have students work in small groups to find examples in the novel. If you want the students to continue recording examples in the remaining chapters, assign a due date for the worksheet.

    Examples from the novel:
the kind who looks like a Saint Bernard puppy, Chapter 1, simile
a grin like a friendly lion, Chapter 1, simile

HYPERBOLE	Extreme exaggeration used to describe a person or thing. For example: *She had as many pairs of shoes as there are stars in the sky.*
IRONY	The use of words to express something different from and often opposite to their literal meaning.
METAPHOR	A comparison without the words like or as. For example, *The cat is a bag of bones*.
METONYMY	A figure of speech in which one word or phrase is substituted for another with which it is closely associated, as in the use of *Washington* for the United States government or of *the sword* for military power.
ONOMATOPOEIA	The use of words such as *buzz* or *splash* that imitate the sounds associated with the objects or actions they refer to.
PARADOX	A seemingly self-contradictory statement that has some truth to it.
PERSONIFICATION	Attributing human characteristics to inanimate objects, animals, or ideas, as in *the wind howled*.
SIMILE	A comparison using the words like or as.

FIGURES OF SPEECH

Figures of speech are literary devices that give the writer a non-literal way to describe images and events. The main types of figures of speech are hyperbole, irony, metaphor, metonymy, onomatopoeia, paradox, personification, and simile. Use the following chart to record examples of figures of speech used in *That Was Then, This Is Now*. A sample has been done for you. Note: You may not find an example of each figure of speech in the novel.

Figure of Speech	Example from Novel, page #	Literal Meaning
simile	I look like a baby-faced kid. p. 1	Bryon looks very young.

LESSON ELEVEN

Student Objectives
1. To discuss the main ideas and events in Chapters 8-9
2. To complete the prereading vocabulary work for Chapters 10-11
3. To preview the study questions for Chapters 10-11
4. To read Chapters 10-11 orally

Activity #1
Give each student four 1"x2" strips of colored paper or index cards--one blue, one yellow, one green, one pink. Have students put a large letter A on the blue paper, B on the yellow, C on the green, and D on the pink. Distribute copies of the Multiple Choice/Quiz questions for Chapters 8-9, or reproduce the page on an overhead transparency and show it. Ask students to read the first question and hold up the colored paper for the correct answer. Continue with the remaining questions.

Activity #2
Write the vocabulary words on the board. Ask students to predict their meanings. Then have students complete the prereading vocabulary worksheet and check their answers.

Activity #3
Go over the study questions with the students and have them predict the answers.

Activity #4
Have volunteers read the chapters aloud to the rest of the class.

LESSON TWELVE

Student Objectives
1. To discuss the main ideas and events in Chapters 10-11
2. To discuss character traits

Activity #1
Go over the answers to the study questions with the students. Have them read the parts of the chapters aloud that support their answers.

Activity #2 Minilesson: Character Traits
Explain that an author creates a main character, in this case Bryon Douglas, by giving him traits such as physical attributes, thoughts, and feelings. The author develops these traits by telling how the character looks as well as what the character says, does, and thinks. Writers usually base their characters at least in part on a real person or persons, and then elaborate. A good writer will make the characters believable for the readers. Minor characters are also developed, although not in as much detail as the main character.

Distribute copies of the Character Traits Chart. Have students work in small groups to complete it. Invite a representative from each group to present their ideas to the class.

If time permits, have each group choose a different minor character and complete a Character Traits Chart for that character.

CHARACTER TRAITS CHART
That Was Then

Character _____

Trait _____	Trait _____	Trait _____	Trait _____
Events That Show It	Events That Show It	Events That Show It	Events That Show It

LESSON THIRTEEN

Student Objectives
    1. To complete the Plot Diagram
    2. To complete a Plot Profile

Activity #1

Work with the class to complete the Plot Diagram. Remind students that the climax is the high point of the story, and that it separates the middle from the end of the story. Discuss all opinions regarding the climax of the story. Have students use examples from the novel to support their opinions. Most should agree that the climax occurs in Chapter Ten, when Bryon calls the police to report Mark's possession of the pills.

Activity #2

A Plot Profile is a method of examining the tension, excitement, conflict, or suspense in a story. Make a copy of the Plot Profile on an overhead transparency, or draw one on the board. Have the class agree on the criteria for each of the levels from 1-10 (1 being low, and 10 high.) Briefly review the events of each chapter, and discuss the amount of tension or excitement in each one. Record students' consensus about each chapter on the Plot Profile. Analyze the Profile when completed. Use questions such as: Where is the tension the highest? Where is it the lowest? Would the story be too stressful without the low points? Was the tension reduced enough at the end?

LESSON FOURTEEN

Objectives:
To discuss the novel on a deeper than direct recall level.

Activity

There are a variety of ways to use the extra discussion questions which follow. You could have students tackle them individually or in groups, as a writing assignment or orally as a whole class activity. Use your own discretion about how to use these questions, considering your particular class.

EXTRA WRITING ASSIGNMENT/DISCUSSION QUESTIONS

Interpretation

1. From what point of view is the story written? How does this affect our understanding of the story?

2. What are the main conflicts in the story? Are they resolved? If so, how? If not, why not?

3. The author does not give a specific setting. What inferences did you make to determine the setting? What clues did the author give? How important is the setting to the story?

4. What are the main themes of the novel?

5. Discuss the roles of one or more of the supporting characters.

6. Why does Charlie let the boys hang out in his bar, when he knows they are minors?

7. Why does Bryon lie so much? (Chapters 2,3)

8. Why does Bryon have difficulty accepting authority? (Chapter 2)

9. What does Mike's reaction to the boys who beat him say about him? (Chapter 2)

10. Why was Bryon in a funny mood on the Monday after Mark's injury? (Chapter 4)

11. Discuss the irony in the incident involving the principal's car. (Chapter 4)

12. In Chapter 5, Bryon says it is a law that parents never know what all their kids are doing. How does the author show this?

13. In Chapter 5, Bryon says he has a very bad ego hang up. How does his ego hang-up affect his later decisions?

14. Bryon and Mark began acting strangely. Bryon thought Mark felt as if something was slipping and he was trying to hang on. He said he was trying to hang on himself. What was happening? (Chapter 5)

15. In Chapter 5, Bryon said he was changing, but Mark was not. Do the events in the story support this statement?

16. In Chapter 5, why was Mark acting strangely?

17. In Chapter 7, Mark says nothing bad ever happened to him. Why would he think this?

18. Why do you think Bryon stopped calling Cathy?

19. Bryon stated that "Mark always comes through everything untouched, unworried, unaffected." Why would Bryon think this?

20. Why did Mark and Cathy dislike each other?

Critical
21. Is the plot of the story believable? Why or why not?

22. How did Bryon change over the course of the novel? Were these changes for the better?

23. Were the characters believable? Why or why not?

24. The author often used vivid language to describe a scene or event. Give an example of her use of vivid language that you found most effective. Tell why it was effective.

25. Discuss the use of foreshadowing in the novel.

26. What was the overall mood of the story? Give examples to support your answer.

27. Why did the author have Charlie die?

28. How does the author create suspense?

29. What is the role/importance of Bryon's mother?

30. What problem or conflict does the author use to get the story started? How effective is it?

31. Could any of the main events be left out? Which ones? Why or why not?

32. Could you change the order of the main events and still have the same outcome? If not, how would the outcome change if the order of the events were changed?

33. How would the story have to change to have a different ending?

34. How would the story change if there were a different narrator?

35. Which character do you know the most about? Which character do you know the least about?

36. Were you able to predict the ending? What clues did the author give?

37. Discuss the author's use of language. Is it natural? Do people you know talk the way the characters did?

38. Does the mood of the story change? How does the author show this? What words does the author use to create the mood or atmosphere of the book?

39. Which chapter was most important? Why?

40. Were the descriptions in the book effective? Give some examples.

41. Which senses did the descriptions cause you to use? Give examples of the descriptions using hearing, seeing, touching, smelling, taste.

42. The narrator compares himself to a Saint Bernard and Mark to a pet lion. Are these descriptions accurate?

43. Explain how the title relates to the events and themes of the novel.

Personal Response

44. Did you enjoy reading *That Was Then, This Is Now*? Why or why not?

45. Is *That Was Then, This Is Now* a good title for the book? Why or why not? If not, what title would you suggest?

46. What do you think Bryon will do next?

47. What do you think Mark will do when he gets out of prison?

48. If you were Bryon, what would you have done when you found the pills under Mark's bed?

49. Did either Bryon's or Mark's experiences change the way you look at yourself? How?

50. If you were Bryon's mother, what would you do to try and help him?

51. Mike Chambers did not want to get even with the boys who beat him up. What would you say if you were discussing this incident with him?

52. What do you think of Mike's father and his reaction to Mike's injury?

53. Do you think Mark supplied the drugs M&M took?

54. Will you read more of S. E. Hinton's books? Why or why not?

55. Did you have strong feelings while reading this book? If so, what did the author do to cause those feelings? If not, why not?

56. Have you read any other stories similar to *That Was Then, This Is Now?* If so, tell about them.

57. Would you recommend this book to another student? Why or why not?

58. What makes S. E. Hinton a unique and different author?

59. What questions would you like to ask S. E. Hinton?

60. What was the saddest part? What was the most exciting part?

61. What do you remember most about the story?

QUOTATIONS

Discuss the significance of the following quotations.

1. "It was a donation," Mark said seriously, "for the Cause."
   "What cause?"
   "Cause we owe it to Charlie," Mark said . . .

2. "You make me sick! You just rescued me from some guys who were going to beat me up because I'm different from them, and now you're going to beat up someone because he's different from you. You think I'm weird-well, you're the weird ones."

3. "Kill the white bastard."

4. "Yeah, I mean it. Man, if anybody ever hurt me like that I'd hate them for the rest of my life."

5. "Bryon, you're an honest kid in most ways, but you lie like a dog. Take Mark--I wouldn't trust him around anything that wasn't nailed down, but I'd believe anything he said. I'd trust you with my wife, if I had one. I trust your actions, but I double-check most of your statements. You just think about it, and I think you'll come up with the reason why you haven't got a job before now. You just think about it/"

6. "You're jealous, Bryon, because Angela dumped you to make a play for Curtis, and he was smart enough to leave her alone."

7. If you have two friends in your lifetime, you're lucky. If you have one *good* friend, you're more than lucky.

8. "I'd forgotten how beautiful he is. I know girls who would give their eye teeth for hair that color."

9. You know what the crummiest feeling you can have is? To hate the person you love best in the world.

10. "Certainly uses nice language. A real lady."

11. "Buddy boy, you are dead. You had just better make up your mind to that. When I get through with you, you are going to be dead."

12. "Y'know, when I first came around tonight, after that kid cracked me, I was scared stiff. I thought I was dyin', I was so scared. I really felt weird. But after I got to thinkin' you were there with me, I calmed down. Bryon, you're the only family I got, you know that? I mean, your mom's been great to me and everything, but I don't feel like she's really *my* old lady. But I feel like you're my brother. A real one.

13. "Do you ever get the feeling that the whole thing is changin'? Like somethin' is coming to an end because somethin' else is beginning?"

14. "The difference is," I said evenly, "that was then, and this is now."

15. That was strange, too: in the past, I thought in terms of "we," now I was thinking in terms of "me."

16. "I wish I was dead--or somebody else."

17. "Not ever. I'm not going home."

18. "Yeah, but M&M is just a kid."
    "So are we. Nothing bad happens to you when you're a kid. Or haven't you realized that?"
    "Youth is free from worry," I said sarcastically. "You've been listenin' to too many adults."
    "I don't worry. I'm never scared of nothing, and I never will be," Mark said, "as long as I'm a kid."
    "You can get away with anything."

19. "I get so sick," Angela was saying. "I feel like I can't take it anymore, life is so lousy. I'm lousy, everything is lousy. I can't stand it at home. I can't stand it at school, I can't stand it anywhere. I always thought, hell, I can get what I want. Get what I want and everybody can go to hell. But it doesn't work that way, Bryon. I'm going to hell right along with them. I'm already there."

20. She would say, "I was sick of all that hot mess." She'd never let on.

21. "I didn't like livin' at home; I got sick of them yelling and fighting all the time. I got whipped a lot, too. I remember thinking, This'll save me the trouble of shooting them myself. I don't like anybody hurtin' me."

22. "You can't walk through your whole life saying 'If.' You can't keep trying to figure out why things happen, man. That s what old people do. That's when you can't get away with things any more. You gotta just take things as they come, and quit trying to reason them out. Bryon, you never used to wonder about things. Man, I been gettin' worried about you. You start wonderin' why, and you get old. Lately, I felt like you were leavin' me, man. You used to have all the answers."

23. "I don't want to keep this up, this getting-even jazz. It's stupid and I'm sick of it and it keeps going in circles. I have had it--so if you're planning any get-even mugging, forget it."

24. "Thanks for letting me use your car, Charlie. Thanks for saving my life."

25. "Baby, what have you done to yourself?"

26. "Bryon, I want to tell you how much I appreciate all you've done. I'm really proud of you, son."

27. "I called the cops."

28. "My God, Bryon, you're not going to let them take me to jail?"

29. "Mom," I said wearily, "what have I done? You don't hate me, do you?"

30. "Bryon, why are you doing this to me?"

31. "Bryon, you got even with Mark for Cathy, then you got even with Cathy for Mark. When are you going to stop getting even with yourself?"

32. "I didn't have to see you. I wanted to, though. I had to make sure."
    "Make sure of what?"
    "Make sure I hated you."

33. "Like a friend once said to me, 'That was then, and this is now.' "

LESSON FIFTEEN

Student Objective
    To practice writing a personal opinion.

Activity #1
    Lead the class in a discussion of Bryon's actions in Chapter 10, when he turned Mark in to the police. Invite opinions about why he did it, and the appropriateness of his actions. Tell students they will have the opportunity to express their opinions in writing.

Activity #2
    Distribute copies of Writing Assignment #3. Give students the rest of the class time to work on it. Set a due date for those who do not finish in class.

PLOT PROFILE
That Was Then, This Is Now

HIGH											
LOW											
CHAPTER	1	2	3	4	5	6	7	8	9	10	11

Discuss your personal reaction to the plot.

Illustrate one of the conflicts in the story.

WRITING ASSIGNMENT #3 *That Was Then*
Expressing a Personal Opinion

PROMPT

Bryon turned Mark in to the police for selling pills. His mother thought Mark's actions were wrong, and that maybe the juvenile authorities could help him. Angela told Bryon she thought what he did to Mark was really low. You have discussed the topic in class. Your assignment is to express your opinion of Bryon's actions in writing.

PREWRITING

Form your opinion. It is probably best to do this without further discussion with classmates. Next, brainstorm a list of reasons for your opinion. Decide on the best order for your reasons, and number them on your list.

DRAFTING

Your opening statement should state the topic and give your opinion about it.. Next state your most important reason. Explain your reason with personal experiences or facts about the topic. In the next paragraph, state your next reason and the facts that support it. Write one paragraph for each reason. In your closing paragraph, state your topic and opinion again.

PEER CONFERENCE/REVISING

When you finish the rough draft, ask another student to look at it. You may want to give the student your brainstorm list so he/she can double check for you and see that you have included all of the information. After reading, he or she should tell you what he/she liked best about your opinion paper, which parts were difficult to understand or needed more information, and ways in which your work could be improved. Reread your opinion paper considering your critic's comments and make the corrections you think are necessary.

PROOFREADING/EDITING

Do a final proofreading of your opinion paper, double-checking your grammar, spelling, organization, and the clarity of your ideas.

FINAL DRAFT

Follow your teacher's directions for making a final copy of your paper.

LESSON SIXTEEN

Student Objective
  To review all of the vocabulary work done in this unit

Activity
  Use one or more of the following vocabulary review activities.

VOCABULARY REVIEW ACTIVITIES

1. Divide your class into two teams and have an old-fashioned spelling or definition bee.

2. Give individuals or groups of students a *That Was Then, This Is Now* Vocabulary Word Search Puzzle. The person (group) to find all of the vocabulary words in the puzzle first wins.

3. Give students a *That Was Then, This Is Now* Vocabulary Word Search Puzzle without the word list. The person or group to find the most vocabulary words in the puzzle wins.

4. Put a *That Was Then, This Is Now* Vocabulary Crossword Puzzle onto a transparency on the overhead projector and do the puzzle together as a class.

5. Give students a *That Was Then, This Is Now* Vocabulary Matching Worksheet to do.

6. Use words from the word jumble page and have students spell them correctly.

7. Have students write a story in which they correctly use as many vocabulary words as possible. Have students read their compositions orally. Post the most original compositions on your bulletin board.

8. Have students work in teams and play charades with the vocabulary words.

9. Select a word of the day and encourage students to use it correctly in their writing and speaking vocabulary.

10. Have a contest to see which students can find the most vocabulary words used in other sources. You may want to have a bulletin board available so the students can write down their word, the sentence it was used in, and the source.

LESSON SEVENTEEN

Objective

    To review the main ideas presented in *That Was Then, This Is Now*

Activity #1

    Choose one of the review games/activities included in the packet and spend your class period as outlined there.

Activity #2

    Remind students of the date for the Unit Test. Stress the review of the Study Guides and their class notes as a last minute, brush-up review for homework.

REVIEW GAMES / ACTIVITIES

1. Ask the class to make up a unit test for *That Was Then, This Is Now*. The test should have 4 sections: multiple choice, true/false, short answer and essay. Students may use 1/2 period to make the test, including a separate answer sheet, and then swap papers and use the other 1/2 class period to take a test a classmate has devised. (open book)

2. Take 1/2 period for students to make up true and false questions (including the answers). Collect the papers and divide the class into two teams. Draw a big tic-tac-toe board on the chalk board. Make one team X and one team O. Ask questions to each side, giving each student one turn. If the question is answered correctly, that student's team's letter (X or O) is placed in the box. If the answer is incorrect, no mark is placed in the box. The object is to get three marks in a row like tic-tac-toe. You may want to keep track of the number of games won for each team.

3. Take 1/2 period for students to make up questions (true/false and short answer). Collect the questions. Divide the class into two teams. You'll alternate asking questions to individual members of teams A & B (like in a spelling bee). The question keeps going from A to B until it is correctly answered, then a new question is asked. A correct answer does not allow the team to get another question. Correct answers are +2 points; incorrect answers are -1 point.

4. Allow students time to quiz each other (in pairs) from their study guides and class notes.

5. Give students a *That Was Then, This Is Now* crossword puzzle to complete.

REVIEW GAMES / ACTIVITIES

6. Divide your class into two teams. Use the *That Was Then, This Is Now* crossword words with their letters jumbled as a word list. Student 1 from Team A faces off against Student 1 from Team B. You write the first jumbled word on the board. The first student (1A or 1B) to unscramble the word wins the chance for his/her team to score points. If 1A wins the jumble, go to student 2A and give him/her a clue. He/she must give you the correct word which matches that clue. If he/she does, Team A scores a point, and you give student 3A a clue for which you expect another correct response. Continue giving Team A clues until some team member makes an incorrect response. An incorrect response sends the game back to the jumbled-word face off, this time with students 2A and 2B. Instead of repeating giving clues to the first few students of each team, continue with the student after the one who gave the last incorrect response on the team.

7. Take on the persona of "The Answer Person." Allow students to ask any question about the book. Answer the questions, or tell students where to look in the book to find the answer.

8. Students may enjoy playing charades with events from the story. Select a student to start. Give him/her a card with a scene or event from the story. Allow the players to use their books to find the scene being described. The first person to guess each charade performs the next one.

9. Play a categories-type quiz game. (A master is included in this Unit Plan). Make an overhead transparency of the categories form. Divide the class into teams of three or four players each. Have each team Choose a recorder and a banker. Choose a team to go first. That team will choose a category and point amount. Ask the question to the entire class.(Use the Study Guide Quiz and Vocabulary questions.) Give the teams one minute to discuss the answer and write it down. Walk around the room and check the answers. Each team that answers correctly receives the points. (Incorrect answers are not penalized; they just don't receive any points). Cross out that square on the playing board. Play continues until all squares have been used. The winning team is the one with the most points. You can assign bonus points to any square or squares you choose.

10. Have individual students draw scenes from the book. Display the scenes and have the rest of the class look in their books to find the chapter or section that is being depicted. The first student to find the correct scene then displays his or her picture. When the game is over, collect the pictures and put them in a binder for students to look at during their free time.

NOTE: If students do not need the extra review, omit this lesson and go on to the test.

LESSON EIGHTEEN

Objective

To test the students' understanding of the main ideas and themes in *That Was Then, This Is Now*

Activity #1

Distribute the Unit Tests for *That Was Then, This Is Now*. Go over the instructions in detail and allow the students the entire class period to complete the exam.

Activity #2

Collect all test papers and assigned books prior to the end of the class period.

NOTES ABOUT THE UNIT TESTS IN THIS UNIT:

There are 5 different unit tests which follow.

There are two short answer tests which are based primarily on facts from the novel. The answer key for short answer unit test 1 follows the student test. The answer key for short answer test 2 follows the student short answer unit test 2.

There is one advanced short answer unit test. It is based on the extra discussion questions. Use the matching key for short answer unit test 2 to check the matching section of the advanced short answer unit test. There is no key for the short answer questions. The answers will be based on the discussions you have had during class.

There are two multiple choice unit tests. Following the two unit tests, you will find an answer sheet on which students should mark their answers. The same answer sheet should be used for both tests; however, students' answers will be different for each test. Following the students' answer sheet for the multiple choice tests you will find your answer keys.

The short answer tests have a vocabulary section. You should choose 10 of the vocabulary words from this unit, read them orally and have the students write them down. Then, either have students write a definition or use the words in sentences. The second part of the vocabulary test is matching.

LESSON NINETEEN

Objectives
    1. To widen the breadth of students' knowledge about the topics discussed or touched upon in *That Was Then, This Is Now*
    2. To check students' non-fiction assignments

Activity

    Ask each student to give a brief oral report about the nonfiction work he/she read for the nonfiction assignment. Your criteria for evaluating this report will vary depending on the level of your students. You may wish for students to give a complete report without using notes of any kind, or you may want students to read directly from a written report, or you may want to do something in between these two extremes. Just make students aware of your criteria in ample time for them to prepare their reports.

    Start with one student's report. After that, ask if anyone else in the class has read on a topic related to the first student's report. If no one has, choose another student at random. After each report, be sure to ask if anyone has a report related to the one just completed. That will help keep a continuity during the discussion of the reports.

LESSON TWENTY

Objectives
    1. To watch a movie version of the novel *That Was Then, This Is Now*
    2. To compare and contrast the movie with the novel

Activity #1

    The movie version of *That Was Then, This Is Now* is available in many video stores, and through educational film distributors. Show the movie in class. Note: Since the movie version differs somewhat from the book, it is recommended to show it after giving the test.

Activity #2

    Discuss the ways in which the movie and the novel were similar and different. Discuss the reasons for the differences. You may want the students to write a short comparison/contrast paper after this discussion, or record their observations on a Venn Diagram chart.

UNIT TESTS

SHORT ANSWER UNIT TEST 1 *That Was Then, This Is Now*

I. <u>Matching/ Identify</u>

_____ 1. Angela
_____ 2. Bryon
_____ 3. Cathy
_____ 4. Charlie
_____ 5. Curtis
_____ 6. father
_____ 7. M&M
_____ 8. Mark
_____ 9. mother
_____ 10. Texans

A. looked like a St. Bernard puppy
B. who looked like a friendly lion
C. unknowing object of Angela's affections
D. got life in prison
E. got a hair cut from Mark
F. M&M's criticized his hair and grades
G. saved Mark and Bryon's lives
H. liked to take care of strays
I. an innocent chick
J. serious, with a wide-eyed, trusting look

II. <u>Short Answer</u>

1. Describe the relationship between Bryon and Mark. Include where they lived, and why.

2. Describe Bryon's visit to his mother while she was in the hospital. Whom did he meet on the way there? Which two people did he meet at the hospital? Summarize his discussions with each of them.

Short Answer Unit Test 1 *That Was Then, This Is Now*

3. Describe the fight at the dance. Tell what happened, and why.

4. Bryon found something under Mark's mattress when he was looking for cigarettes. What was it? What did Bryon do after he found it? What were the results of Bryon's actions?

5. Discuss the significance of the following quotation: "Do you ever get the feeling that the whole thing is changin'? Like somethin' is coming to an end because somethin' else is beginning?"

Short Answer Unit Test 1 *That Was Then, This Is Now*

III. Fill in the Blanks

Directions: Write the word or words to correctly complete each sentence about the story.

1. Bryon's girlfriend, Cathy, had a younger brother named _____.

2. One night while they were all driving along _____, he got out of the car.

3. He went to live with some _____.

4. They called him _____.

5. While he was there, he _____.

6. When Bryon and Cathy found him, he was _____.

7. They took him to the _____.

8. Mr. Carlson thanked Bryon for his help and called him "_____."

9. The young boy recovered, but his _____ was gone.

10. Bryon's anger about this incident later led to a major conflict with _____.

IV. Essay
    Discuss the meaning and significance of the title, *That Was Then, This Is Now*.

Short Answer Unit Test 1 *That Was Then, This Is Now*

V. Vocabulary

Listen to the vocabulary words and spell them. After you have spelled all the words, go back and write down the definitions.

WORD **DEFINITION**

1. _____ _____
2. _____ _____
3. _____ _____
4. _____ _____
5. _____ _____
6. _____ _____
7. _____ _____
8. _____ _____
9. _____ _____
10. _____ _____

Vocabulary Part 2   Directions: Place the letter of the matching definition on the blank line.

_____ 1. profound   A. unclear
_____ 2. inclined   B. slowed
_____ 3. contorted   C. likely or tending to
_____ 4. sauntered   D. slipping back
_____ 5. incredulous   E. twisted out of shape
_____ 6. relapse   F. intellectual
_____ 7. obscure   G. seriously
_____ 8. witticism   H. strolled
_____ 9. gravely   I. joke
_____ 10. slacked   J. doubtful

ANSWER KEY SHORT ANSWER UNIT TEST 1 *That Was Then, This Is Now*

I. Matching/Identify

E	1.	Angela	A.	looked like a St. Bernard puppy
A	2.	Bryon	B.	who looked like a friendly lion
I	3.	Cathy	C.	unknowing object of Angela's affections
G	4.	Charlie	D.	got life in prison
C	5.	Curtis	E.	got a hair cut from Mark
F	6.	father	F.	M&M's criticized his hair and grades
J	7.	M&M	G.	saved Mark and Bryon's lives
B	8.	Mark	H.	liked to take care of strays
H	9.	mother	I.	an innocent chick
D	10.	Texans	J.	serious, with a wide-eyed, trusting look

1. Describe the relationship between Bryon and Mark. Include where they lived, and why.

    Mark lived with Bryon and his mother. Mark's parents had shot and killed each other several years earlier, when he was 9 and Bryon was 10, and Mark had lived with them ever since.

    They are like brothers. They have been friends for years, even before Mark came to live at Bryon's house. Mark considers Bryon his only family.

2. Describe Bryon's visit to his mother while she was in the hospital. Whom did he meet on the way there? Which two people did he meet at the hospital? Summarize his discussions with each of them.

    Randy was a hippie college student who drove a Volkswagen bus. He picked the boys up when they were hitching a ride to the hospital. He also told them about the house where he lived.

    Bryon's mother asked him to visit a boy in the hospital across the hall from her room. His name was Mike Chambers. He was in the hospital because he had been beaten up. He had stopped to help a black girl who was being harassed by a group of white boys. He drove her home. When he got to her house, a group of black boys surrounded the car. They asked her what they should do with him, and she said to kill him. The black boys beat him up, and he was in the hospital recovering. Mike said his father told him he was dumb.

    Bryon went to the snack bar at the hospital. Cathy was working there, and recognized him, although he did not recognize her at first. Then he told her he wanted to talk to her sometime, and she agreed.

3. Describe the fight at the dance. Tell what happened, and why.

    Mark was trying to protect Curtis from a an attacker. The attacker turned on Mark and hit him over the head with a bottle. By the time Bryon got to the scene, the police were there and had the boy in handcuffs. Bryon told the boy he would kill him. Then Bryon saw Angela talking to the boy and surmised that she had asked the boy to attack Curtis to get even with him because he was not interested in her. He changed his mind, and decided to get even with her instead of the boy. He asked Curtis if he knew Angela, and Curtis said no. Then Bryon went to the hospital with Mark.

    Curtis hot-wired Charlie's car and drove Cathy to the hospital. Bryon put Mark in the back seat, then dropped Cathy off. He didn't kiss her, because the porch light was on, and her little brothers and sisters were looking out the window. He said he would call her.

4. Bryon found something under Mark's mattress when he was looking for cigarettes. What was it? What did Bryon do after he found it? What were the results of Bryon's actions?

    Bryon looked under Mark's mattress. He found a cylinder of pills. He realized Mark was selling drugs. He called the police and reported Mark.

    Bryon told Mark he had called the police. Mark reminded Bryon what it could do to him, since he already had a record. When the police came, he stood quivering as Bryon told the police all he knew.

    Mark got five years in the state reformatory. Bryon thought the judge went hard on him because of his bad attitude.

5. Discuss the significance of the following quotation: "Do you ever get the feeling that the whole thing is changin'? Like somethin' is coming to an end because somethin' else is beginning?"

    The day after the fight, Mark was still not feeling much better. He and Bryon stayed home. They reminisced about the things they did when they were little kids. Then they talked about the way things were changing. Mark wondered why there was a difference, and Bryon said it was because, "that was then ,and this is now."

I

II. Fill in the Blanks

1. Bryon's girlfriend, Cathy, had a younger brother named **M&M.**
2. One night while they were all driving along **The Ribbon**, he got out of the car.
3. He went to live with some **hippies in a large house.**
4. They called him **Baby Freak.**
5. While he was there, he **took drugs**.
6. When Bryon and Cathy found him, he was **on a bad trip from LSD.**.
7. They took him to the **hospital**.
8. Mr. Carlson thanked Bryon for his help and called him "**son**."
9. The young boy recovered, but his **memory** was gone.
10. Bryon's anger about this incident later led to a major conflict with **Mark**.

IV. Essay Answers will vary depending on your class discussions and the level of your students. Grade the essays on your own criteria.

Answer Key Short Answer Unit Test 1 *That Was Then, This Is Now*

V. Vocabulary Choose ten words to dictate for this part of the test.

Vocabulary Part 2

F	1.	profound	A.	unclear
C	2.	inclined	B.	slowed
E	3.	contorted	C.	likely or tending to
H	4.	sauntered	D.	slipping back
J	5.	incredulous	E.	twisted out of shape
D	6.	relapse	F.	intellectual
A	7.	obscure	G.	seriously
I	8.	witticism	H.	strolled
G	9.	gravely	I.	joke
B	10.	slacked	J.	doubtful

SHORT ANSWER UNIT TEST 2 *That Was Then, This Is Now*

I. <u>Matching/ Identify</u>

_____ 1.	Saint Bernard	A.	Mark's drug-selling sentence
_____ 2.	friendly lion	B.	Texans' murder sentence
_____ 3.	Sir Galahad	C.	Mark's real father
_____ 4.	stupid	D.	Mr. Chambers thought this of his son
_____ 5.	hustling	E.	resemblance to Mark
_____ 6.	hot-wiring	F.	Mark's "talent"
_____ 7.	cowboy	G.	resemblance to Bryon
_____ 8.	probation	H.	Mark's car theft sentence
_____ 9.	five years	I.	Bryon's "talent"
_____ 10.	life	J.	resemblance to Mike

II. <u>Short Answer</u>

1. Discuss the relationships between Bryon and Mark, Bryon and Cathy, and Mark and Cathy.

2. Mark and Bryon hustled two men in the bar. What happened after they left the bar? Include all details, in order.

Short Answer Unit Test 2 *That Was Then, This Is Now*

3. Bryon said Mark was acting strange. What was he doing?

4. Describe the last meeting between Bryon and Mark. How did Bryon feel at the end of the story?

5. Discuss the significance of the following quotation: "I called the cops."

Short Answer Unit Test 2 *That Was Then, This Is Now*

III. Fill in the Blank
Directions: Write the word or words to correctly complete each sentence about the story.

1. While at the dance, Mark was trying to protect _____ from a boy who was attacking him.
2. The attacker turned on Mark and _____ him with _____.
3. Bryon got to the scene and saw _____ talking to the boy. Then he knew who had set up the attack, and why.
4. _____ has set up the attack because _____ was not interested in having a dating relationship.
5. Later, Mark wanted to get even. He did this by _____.
6. The cycle of getting even continued the next day, when _____ and
7. _____ and two other boys beat up
8. _____ while he was waiting in front of Terry Jones's house.
9. _____ wanted to get even for the beating, but
10. _____ did not. This disagreement was only one sign of a growing distance between the two friends.

IV. Essay What are the main themes in the novel. Briefly discuss each.

Short Answer Unit Test 2 *That Was Then, This Is Now*

V. Vocabulary

Listen to the vocabulary words and spell them. After you have spelled all the words, go back and write down the definitions.

	WORD	**DEFINITION**
1.	_____	_____
2.	_____	_____
3.	_____	_____
4.	_____	_____
5.	_____	_____
6.	_____	_____
7.	_____	_____
8.	_____	_____
9.	_____	_____
10.	_____	_____

Vocabulary Part 2 Directions: Place the letter of the matching definition on the blank line.

_____ 1. smirking   A. moved in a bouncing or lively manner
_____ 2. obligingly   B. single; only
_____ 3. irrationally   C. willingly
_____ 4. flounced   D. suddenly
_____ 5. gulf   E. not logically
_____ 6. sassy   F. indistinct
_____ 7. vague   G. sneering
_____ 8. sole   H. distance
_____ 9. lanky   I. tall and skinny
_____ 10. abruptly   J. rude

ANSWER KEY SHORT ANSWER UNIT TEST 2 *That Was Then, This Is Now*

I. <u>Matching/ Identify</u>

Note: Use this key for the Advanced Short Answer Test as well.

G	1.	Saint Bernard	A.	Mark's drug-selling sentence
E	2.	friendly lion	B.	Texans' murder sentence
J	3.	Sir Galahad	C.	Mark's real father
D	4.	stupid	D.	Mr. Chambers thought this of his son
I	5.	hustling	E.	resemblance to Mark
F	6	hot-wiring	F.	Mark's "talent"
C	7.	cowboy	G.	resemblance to Bryon
H	8.	probation	H.	Mark's car theft sentence
A	9.	five years	I.	Bryon's "talent"
B	10.	life	J.	resemblance to Mike

II. <u>Short Answer</u>

1. Discuss the relationships between Bryon and Mark, Bryon and Cathy, and Mark and Cathy.

    Bryon and Mark are like brothers. They have been friends for years, even before Mark came to live at Bryon's house. Cathy is Bryon's girlfriend. They like each other, but he wants her to be crazy about him. Bryon felt sick and mad and hot and cold all at once when, at a dance, Cathy said Mark was beautiful. Mark and Cathy did not get along well. They seemed to be vying for Bryon's affection.

2. Mark and Bryon hustled two men in the bar. What happened after they left the bar? Include all details, in order.

    The two Texans left the bar first. They stepped out of the alley next to the bar as the boys came out. Dirty Dave told them to step into the alley, and that he had a gun. The other one took the gun while Dirty Dave put on some brass knuckles. Mark told them they would know if they tackled with him. He used a voice that Bryon didn't recognize. Just then Charlie stepped into the alley and told them to put the gun down, because he was carrying a sawed-off shotgun. The Texans put the gun down and the boys walked past. Then one of the Texans reached for the gun and fired at them. Charlie slammed them to the ground. Mark grabbed the gun Charlie had dropped, and fired back at the Texans as they climbed over the wall. Bryon told Charlie he could get off of him, and the boys realized that Charlie had been shot above the eye, and was dead.

3. Bryon said Mark was acting strange. What was he doing?

    He would stare at Bryon for long periods of time. It seemed to Bryon that Mark was trying to figure out who he (Bryon) was. Sometimes he acted jealous of Cathy.

Answer Key Short Answer Unit Test 2 *That Was Then, This Is Now*

4. Describe the last meeting between Bryon and Mark. How did Bryon feel at the end of the story?

   Bryon went to the reformatory. He tried to apologize. Mark said when he got out he was leaving and Bryon would never see him again. Bryon reminded him that they had been like brothers. Mark reminded Bryon that he had once said, "That was then, and this is now."

   At the end of the story, Bryon said he was too mixed up to care. He wished he could be a kid again, when he had all of the answers.

5. Discuss the significance of the following quotation: "I called the cops."

   Bryon looked under Mark's mattress for cigarettes. Instead, he found a cylinder of pills. He realized Mark was selling drugs. He called the police and reported Mark.

   When Mark got home, Bryon told him he had called the police. Mark reminded Bryon what it could do to him, since he already had a record. When the police came, he stood quivering as Bryon told the police all he knew.

III. Fill in the Blank

1. While at the dance, Mark was trying to protect **Curtis** from a boy who was attacking him.
2. The attacker turned on Mark and **hit** him with **a bottle**.
3. Bryon got to the scene and saw **Angela** talking to the boy. Then he knew who had set up the attack, and why.
4. **Angela** had set up the attack because **Curtis** was not interested in having a dating relationship.
5. Later, Mark wanted to get even. He did this by **cutting off Angela's long hair**.
6. The cycle of getting even continued the next day, when **Tim** and
7. **Curly Shephard** and two other boys beat up
8. **Bryon** while he was waiting in front of Terry Jones's house.
9. **Mark** wanted to get even for the beating, but
10. Bryon did not. This disagreement was only one sign of a growing distance between the two friends.

IV. Essay Answers will vary depending on your class discussions and the level of your class.

V. <u>Vocabulary</u>   Choose ten words to dictate for this portion of the test.

<u>Vocabulary Part 2</u>

G	1.	smirking	A.	moved in a bouncing or lively manner
C	2.	obligingly	B.	single; only
E	3.	irrationally	C.	willingly
A	4.	flounced	D.	suddenly
H	5.	gulf	E.	not logically
J	6.	sassy	F.	indistinct
F	7.	vague	G.	sneering
B	8.	sole	H.	distance
I	9.	lanky	I.	tall and skinny
D	10.	abruptly	J.	rude

ADVANCED SHORT ANSWER UNIT TEST *That Was Then, This Is Now*

I. <u>Matching/ Identify</u>

1.	Saint Bernard	A.	Mark's drug-selling sentence
2.	friendly lion	B.	Texans' murder sentence
3.	Sir Galahad	C.	Mark's real father
4.	stupid	D.	Mr. Chambers thought this of his son
5.	hustling	E.	resemblance to Mark
6	hot-wiring	F.	Mark's "talent"
7.	cowboy	G.	resemblance to Bryon
8.	probation	H.	Mark's car theft sentence
9.	five years	I.	Bryon's "talent"
10.	life	J.	resemblance to Mike

II. Short Answer

1. Explain how the title relates to the events and themes of the novel.

2. Discuss the relationships between Bryon and Mark, Bryon and Cathy, and Mark and Cathy. How did these different relationships influence Bryon and affect his decisions throughout the story?

Advanced Short Answer Unit Test *That Was Then, This Is Now*

3. Discuss the irony in the incident involving the principal's car.

4. Does the mood of the story change? How does the author show this? What words does the author use to create the mood or atmosphere of the book?

5. Discuss the role of one of the following minor characters: Bryon's mother, Cathy, M&M, Charlie, or Angela.

Advanced Short Answer Unit Test *That Was Then, This Is Now*

III. Quotations

Discuss the significance of the following quotations.

1. "You make me sick! You just rescued me from some guys who were going to beat me up because I'm different from them, and now you're going to beat up someone because he's different from you. You think I'm weird-well, you're the weird ones."

2. "Do you ever get the feeling that the whole thing is changin'? Like somethin' is coming to an end because somethin' else is beginning?"

3. "I get so sick. "I feel like I can't take it anymore, life is so lousy. I'm lousy, everything is lousy. I can't stand it at home. I can't stand it at school, I can't stand it anywhere. I always thought, hell, I can get what I want. Get what I want and everybody can go to hell. But it doesn't work that way, Bryon. I'm going to hell right along with them. I'm already there."

Advanced Short Answer Unit Test *That Was Then, This Is Now*

4. "Yeah, I mean it. Man, if anybody ever hurt me like that I'd hate them for the rest of my life."

5. "I didn't have to see you. I wanted to, though. I had to make sure."
"Make sure of what?"
"Make sure I hated you."

Advanced Short Answer Unit Test *That Was Then, This Is Now*

IV. Vocabulary

Listen to the words and write them down. After you have written down all of the words, write a paragraph in which you use all of the words. The paragraph must in some way relate to *That Was Then, This Is Now*.

1. _____   6. _____
2. _____   7. _____
3. _____   8. _____
4. _____   9. _____
5. _____   10. _____

MULTIPLE CHOICE UNIT TEST 1 *That Was Then, This Is Now*

I. <u>Matching/ Identify</u>

____	1. Angela	A.	looked like a St. Bernard puppy
____	2. Bryon	B.	who looked like a friendly lion
____	3. Cathy	C.	unknowing object of Angela's affections
____	4. Charlie	D.	got life in prison
____	5. Curtis	E.	got a hair cut from Mark
____	6. father	F.	M&M's criticized his hair and grades
____	7. M&M	G.	saved Mark and Bryon's lives
____	8. Mark	H.	liked to take care of strays
____	9. mother	I.	an innocent chick
____	10. Texans	J.	serious, with a wide-eyed, trusting look

II. <u>Multiple Choice</u>

1. Bryon and Mark saved someone from being jumped, and now they were going to do the same thing to someone else. This person said their attitude made them sick. Who was it?
    A. It was Bryon's mother.
    B. It was M&M.
    C. It was Curtis.
    D. It was Douglas.

2. How did Bryon describe the relationship between himself and Mark?
    A. They were casual acquaintances.
    B. They used to be friends, but weren't any more.
    C. They were good friends.
    D. They were like brothers.

3. What did Bryon learn about Mike Chambers?
    A. A group of black boys beat him up after he helped a black girl.
    B. He had been in jail for hitting someone over the head with a bottle.
    C. He lived in a commune and studied English at the local college.
    D. He wanted to marry Bryon's mother.

4. What made Bryon feel hot and cold and sick and mad, all at once, for a second?
    A. Mark made a pass at Cathy.
    B. Cathy said Mark was beautiful.
    C. Cathy told Bryon he was not good enough for her.
    D. Angela told Cathy that Bryon was not a good choice for a boyfriend.

Multiple Choice Unit Test 1 *That Was Then, This Is Now*

5. What happened to Mark at the dance, and why?
    A. He got caught trying to steal liquor from a car in the school parking lot. The owner of the car beat him up.
    B. He was not properly dressed for the dance and was not allowed in.
    C. A cute girl asked him to dance. She picked his pocket while they were dancing, then left him. Later he learned that Curly had set him up.
    D. Mark was trying to protect Curtis from a boy who was attacking him. The attacker turned on Mark and hit him over the head with a bottle.

6. Describe Bryon's mood on the Monday after the dance.
    A. He was the happiest he had been in a long time. He felt like the future held good things for him.
    B. He could hardly concentrate on his school work. He thought about suicide.
    C. He was very angry. He felt like smashing things and beating people up.
    D. He was in a funny mood. He felt like he was standing apart from the others and watching. He felt like he could see through them. It was weird.

7. Bryon told Mark he couldn't help something. What was it?
    A. He couldn't help falling in love with Cathy.
    B. He couldn't help missing Charlie.
    C. He couldn't help thinking about things.
    D. He couldn't help worrying about his mother and his future.

8. What did Bryon find when he looked for Mark's cigarettes?
    A. He found an envelope full of money.
    B. He found ten gold watches.
    C. He found a cylinder of pills.
    D. He found a tin can full of marijuana.

9. Which of the following did **not** happen to M&M?
    A. He cut his hair.
    B. His father kicked him out of the house permanently.
    C. His old expression of trust and intent interest was gone.
    D. His grades were poor.

10. What did Mark tell Bryon he would do when he got out of the reformatory?
    A. Mark said he would get even with Bryon.
    B. Mark said he wanted things to go back to the way they were.
    C. Mark said he wanted to reform and live a clean life.
    D. Mark said when he got out he was leaving and Bryon would never see him again.

Multiple Choice Unit Test 1 *That Was Then, This Is Now*

III. Quotations Write the letter of the word or phrase that completes the quotation.

1. "You make me sick! You just rescued me from some guys who were going to beat me up because I'm different from them, and now you're going to beat up someone because he's different from you. . . .

2. "Yeah, I mean it. Man, if anybody ever hurt me like that . . .

3. "The difference is . . .

4. "Thanks for letting me use your car, Charlie. . .

5. "Mom," I said wearily, "what have I done? . . .

6. Man, I been gettin' worried about you. You start wonderin' why . . .

7. "My God, Bryon, you're not going to. . .

8. "Not ever . . .

9. "You know what the crummiest feeling you can have is?

10. "Nothing bad happens to you. . .

===

A. . . . that was then, and this is now."

B. . . . You don't hate me, do you?"

C. . . . and you get old."

D. . . . I'm not going home."

E. . . . when you're a kid."

F. . . . You think I'm weird-well, you're the weird ones."

G. . . . To hate the person you love best in the world."

H. . . . Thanks for saving my life."

I. . . . I'd hate them for the rest of my life."

J. . . . let them take me to jail?"

Multiple Choice Unit Test 1 *That Was Then, This Is Now*

IV. Vocabulary

___ 1. profound	A.	unclear
___ 2. inclined	B.	slowed
___ 3. contorted	C.	likely or tending to
___ 4. irrationally	D.	single; only
___ 5. incredulous	E.	twisted out of shape
___ 6. sole	F.	intellectual
___ 7. obscure	G.	seriously
___ 8. witticism	H.	not logically
___ 9. gravely	I.	joke
___ 10. slacked	J.	doubtful

Vocabulary Part 2

11. **said before**
    a. taunting
    b. aforementioned
    c. profound
    d. pleading

12. **insulting**
    a. gravely
    b. taunting
    c. vague
    d. vengeful

13. **remembering past events**
    a. vengeful
    b. taunting
    c. reminiscing
    d. pleading

14. **one who is under the legal age**
    a. lame
    b. sole
    c. inclined
    d. minor

15. **slipping back**
    a. aforementioned
    b. sauntered
    c. relapse
    d. taunting

16. **strolled**
    a. sauntered
    b. lame
    c. contorted
    d. slacked

17. **indistinct**
    a. abruptly
    b. vague
    c. sole
    d. slight

18. **sneering**
    a. sinister
    b. sassy
    c. vague
    d. smirking

19. **willingly**
    a. obligingly
    b. abruptly
    c. irrationally
    d. tactfully

20. **supervised freedom for lawbreakers**
    a. commune
    b. probation
    c. hub
    d. gulf

MULTIPLE CHOICE UNIT TEST 2 *That Was Then, This Is Now*

I. <u>Matching/ Identify</u>

_____ 1. Saint Bernard
_____ 2. friendly lion
_____ 3. Sir Galahad
_____ 4. stupid
_____ 5. hustling
_____ 6 hot-wiring
_____ 7. cowboy
_____ 8. probation
_____ 9. five years
_____ 10. life

A. Mark's drug-selling sentence
B. Texans' murder sentence
C. Mark's real father
D. Mr. Chambers thought this of his son
E. resemblance to Mark
F. Mark's "talent"
G. resemblance to Bryon
H. Mark's car theft sentence
I. Bryon's "talent"
J. resemblance to Mike

II. <u>Multiple Choice</u>

1. True or False: Mark lived with Bryon and his mother.
    A. True
    B. False

2. Which of the following does **not** describe M&M?
    A. He was very serious, with a wide-eyed, trusting look on his face.
    B. He wore an old army jacket, moccasins, and a peace symbol around his neck.
    C. He was eleven years old.
    D. He had grey eyes and long, charcoal colored hair.

3. True or False: Curly had a grudge against Bryon because Bryon got the girl Curly wanted.
    A. True
    B. False

4. What happened while Bryon was visiting his mother in the hospital?
    A. He met his mother's boss.
    B. He met Cathy.
    C. He got offered a part-time job.
    D. He was attacked by a security dog and had to get stitches and a rabies shot.

5. Charlie said Bryon was honest in most ways, except one. In what area was Bryon dishonest?
    A. Bryon stole things.
    B. Bryon cheated in school.
    C. Bryon lied a lot.
    D. Bryon mistreated his girlfriends.

Multiple Choice Unit Test 2 *That Was Then, This Is Now*

6. How did Bryon and Mark spend the afternoon after Mark's injury?
    A. Bryon took Mark to the doctor's office for an examination.
    B. They reminisced and talked about the way things were changing.
    C. They hung out at Charlie's.
    D. They drove around looking for Curly and Angela.

7. What happened to Charlie during the fight with the Texans?
    A. He was killed.
    B. He was wounded in the leg. The injury got him out of the draft.
    C. Nothing. Mark saved his life.
    D. He was arrested for possessing an illegal weapon.

8. What did M&M do while they were out driving around?
    A. He got drunk.
    B. He asked them to let him out of the car, and said he was never going home again.
    C. He picked up a girl.
    D. He hid on the floor of the back seat because he didn't like what they were doing.

9. What did Bryon do to get and keep a job?
    A. He cut his hair and shaved.
    B. He begged Charlie for a reference.
    C. He lied about his age on the application.
    D. He stopped saying smart-aleck things, even though he still thought them.

10. Mark said he had never worried about something before. What was it?
    A. He had never worried about his future.
    B. He had never worried about not having a real family.
    C. He had never worried about 'what if?'
    D. He had never worried about his health.

Multiple Choice Unit Test 2 *That Was Then, This Is Now*

III. Quotations Write the letter of the word or phrase that completes the quotation.

1. "Do you ever get the feeling that the whole thing is changin'?

2. "Bryon, you're an honest kid in most ways. . . .

3. "I'd forgotten how beautiful he is.

4. "Bryon, you're . . .

5. "I wish I was dead. . .

6. "I don't worry. I'm never scared of nothing, and I never will be . . .

7. "You can't walk through your whole life saying . . .

8. "My God, Bryon . . .

9. "Like a friend once said to me . . .

10. "Baby . . .
===
A. . . . I know girls who would give their eye teeth for hair that color."

B. . . 'If.' "

C. . . . or somebody else."

D. . . . Like somethin' is coming to an end because somethin' else is beginning?"

E. . . . 'That was then, and this is now.' "

F. . . . as long as I'm a kid."

G. . . . what have you done to yourself?"

H. . . . but you lie like a dog."

I. . . . not going to let them take me to jail?"
J. . . . the only family I got, you know that?"

Multiple Choice Unit Test 2 *That Was Then, This Is Now*

IV. <u>Vocabulary</u>

___ 1.	smirking	A.	moved in a bouncing or lively manner
___ 2.	obligingly	B.	single; only
___ 3.	irrationally	C.	willingly
___ 4.	flounced	D.	suddenly
___ 5.	gulf	E.	not logically
___ 6.	sassy	F.	indistinct
___ 7.	vague	G.	sneering
___ 8.	sole	H.	distance
___ 9.	lanky	I.	tall and skinny
___ 10.	abruptly	J.	rude

<u>Vocabulary Part 2</u>

11. **said before**
    a. taunting
    b. aforementioned
    c. profound
    d. pleading

12. **joke**
    a. hysterical
    b. smirking
    c. witticism
    d. sassy

13. **insulting**
    a. gravely
    b. taunting
    c. vague
    d. vengeful

14. **having an injured leg or foot**
    a. sassy
    b. lame
    c. contorted
    d. slacked

15. **doubtful**
    a. aforementioned
    b. contorted
    c. incredulous
    d. taunting

16. **attack**
    a. commune
    b. vengeful
    c. sinister
    d. assault

17. **willingly**
    a. abruptly
    b. obligingly
    c. sole
    d. slight

18. **sneering**
    a. sinister
    b. sassy
    c. vague
    d. smirking

19. **remembering past events**
    a. vengeful
    b. taunting
    c. reminiscing
    d. pleading

20. **supervised freedom for lawbreakers**
    a. commune
    b. probation
    c. hub
    d. gulf

ANSWER SHEET Multiple Choice Unit Tests
That Was Then, This Is Now

I. Matching

1. _____
2. _____
3. _____
4. _____
5. _____
6. _____
7. _____
8. _____
9. _____
10. _____

III. Quotations

1. _____
2. _____
3. _____
4. _____
5. _____
6. _____
7. _____
8. _____
9. _____
10. _____

IV. Vocabulary

1. _____
2. _____
3. _____
4. _____
5. _____
6. _____
7. _____
8. _____
9. _____
10. _____

Part 2

11. _____
12. _____
13. _____
14. _____
15. _____
16. _____
17. _____
18. _____
19. _____
20.

II. Multiple Choice

1. (A) (B) (C) (D)
2. (A) (B) (C) (D)
3. (A) (B) (C) (D)
4. (A) (B) (C) (D)
5. (A) (B) (C) (D)
6. (A) (B) (C) (D)
7. (A) (B) (C) (D)
8. (A) (B) (C) (D)
9. (A) (B) (C) (D)
10. (A) (B) (C) (D)

ANSWER SHEET KEY   Multiple Choice Unit Test 1 *That Was Then, This Is Now*

I. Matching	III. Quotations	IV. Vocabulary
1. E	1. F	1. F
2. A	2. I	2. C
3. I	3. A	3. E
4. G	4. H	4. H
5. C	5. B	5. J
6. F	6. C	6. D
7. J	7. J	7. A
8. B	8. D	8. I
9. H	9. G	9. G
10. D	10. E	10. B

II. Multiple Choice

1. (A) ( ) (C) (D)
2. (A) (B) (C) ( )
3. ( ) (B) (C) (D)
4. (A) ( ) (C) (D)
5. (A) (B) (C) ( )
6. (A) (B) (C) ( )
7. (A) (B) ( ) (D)
8. (A) (B) ( ) (D)
9. (A) ( ) (C) (D)
10. (A) (B) (C) ( )

Part 2

11. B
12. B
13. C
14. D
15. C
16. A
17. B
18. D
19. A
20. B

ANSWER SHEET KEY   Multiple Choice Unit Test 2

I. Matching

1. G
2. E
3. J
4. D
5. I
6. F
7. C
8. H
9. A
10. B

II. Multiple Choice

1. ( ) (B) (C) (D)
2. (A) (B) ( ) (D)
3. (A) ( ) (C) (D)
4. (A) ( ) (C) (D)
5. (A) (B) ( ) (D)
6. (A) ( ) (C) (D)
7. ( ) (B) (C) (D)
8. (A) ( ) (C) (D)
9. (A) (B) (C) ( )
10. (A) (B) ( ) (D)

III. Quotations

1. D
2. H
3. A
4. I
5. C
6. F
7. B
8. I
9. E
10. G

IV. Vocabulary

1. G
2. C
3. E
4. A
5. H
6. J
7. F
8. B
9. I
10. D

Part 2

11. B
12. C
13. B
14. B
15. C
16. D
17. B
18. D
19. C
20. B

UNIT RESOURCES

BULLETIN BOARD IDEAS

1. Save one corner of the board for the best of students '*That Was Then, This Is Now* writing assignments. You may want to use background photos or pictures to represent the setting of the novel.

2. Take one of the word search puzzles from the extra activities packet and with a marker copy it over in a large size on the bulletin board. Write the clue words to find to one side. Invite students prior to and after class to find the words and circle them on the bulletin board.

3. Have students find or draw pictures that they think resemble the people in the book.

4. Invite students to help make an interactive bulletin board quiz. Give each student a half-sheet of paper (about 4"x5') folded in half so that it can open. On the outside flap, have each student write a description of one of the characters in the text. On the inside, they will write the name of the character. You can staple or tack these papers to the bulletin board so that the students can read the descriptions and lift the flaps to find the answers.

5. Make a display of pictures of book jackets from the various editions of *That Was Then, This Is Now*. You may want to include pictures from the movie.

6. Have students design postcards depicting the settings of the book.

7. Copy one of the quotations and illustrate it.

8. Have students bring pictures or artifacts that remind them of the book. Display them.

9. Have students design a bulletin board (ready to be put up; not just sketched).

10. Have students design a book cover (front and back and inside flaps) for *That Was Then, This Is Now*

EXTRA ACTIVITIES *That Was Then, This Is Now*

One of the difficulties in teaching a novel is that all students don't read at the same speed. One student who likes to read may take the book home and finish it in a day or two. Sometimes a few students finish the in-class assignments early. The problem, then, is finding suitable extra activities for students.

One thing that helps is to keep a little library in the classroom. For this unit on *That Was Then, This Is Now,* you might check out from the school or public library other books by S. E. Hinton. There are also many other similar novels that students would enjoy reading. Several journals and Internet sources have critiques of Hinton's works. Some of the students may enjoy reading these and responding either in writing or in discussion groups.

Your students who have reading difficulties, or speak English as a second language may benefit from listening to all or part of the book on tape.

Other things you may keep on hand are word search puzzles. Several puzzles relating directly to *That Was Then, This Is Now* are included in the unit. Feel free to duplicate them.

Some students may like to draw. You might devise a contest or allow some extra-credit grade for students who draw characters or scenes from *That Was Then, This Is Now*. Note, too, that if the students do not want to keep their drawings you may pick up some extra bulletin board materials this way. If you have a contest and you supply the prize. You could, possibly, make the drawing itself a non-refundable entry fee.

Have maps, a globe, and travel brochures on hand for easy reference. Travel agencies and automobile clubs are good sources for these materials.

The pages which follow contain games, puzzles, and worksheets. The keys, when appropriate, immediately follow the puzzle or worksheet. There are two main groups of activities: one group for the unit; that is, generally relating to the *That Was Then, This Is Now* text, and another group of activities related strictly to the vocabulary.

Directions for the games, puzzles, and worksheets are self-explanatory. The object here is to provide you with extra materials you may use in any way you choose.

MORE ACTIVITIES *That Was Then, This Is Now*

1. Pick one of the incidents for students to dramatize. Encourage students to write dialog for the characters. (Perhaps you could assign various stories to different groups of students so more than one story could be acted and more students could participate.)

2. Use some of the related topics (noted earlier for an in-class library) as topics for research, reports, or written papers, or as topics for guest speakers.

3. Help students design and produce a talk show. Choose one of the story incidents as the topic. The host will interview the various characters. (Students should make up the questions they want the host to ask the characters.)

4. Have students work in pairs to create an interview with one of the characters. One student should be the interviewer and the other should be the interviewee. Students can work together to compose questions for the interviewer to ask. Each pair of students could present their interview to the class.

5. Invite students who have read other books by S. E. Hinton to present booktalks.

6. Invite students who have read a biography of Hinton to tell the class about her life.

7. Have students hold small group discussions related to topics in the book. Assign a recorder and a speaker for each group. Have the speaker from each group make a report to the class.

8. Cast current movie and film stars in the roles of the characters. Defend the choices.

9. Have students work in small groups to write a sequel telling what happened to Bryon and Mark.

10. Write critiques of the book and present them to the class.

11. Write a different ending for the book.

12. Make a comic book version to share with younger readers.

13. Make a collage based on events in the book.

14. Make a diorama or mobile showing the important events from the story.

15. Write and perform a radio or television commercial to advertise the book.

WORD SEARCH *That Was Then*

```
B P A B J G X E A K T E K A B T T O P E L Q K S G I Y G O
V E D M T O T L G K Y C Y U W T J T X V R A R N Q N B P T
D G B P A T I L V V S N K T R H P J L U E E V K O O Q Q T
Y T Q D E E K P S D C A H H A O Z J P J F J Q C M I U F W
X U I V X K F U B T O D O O O P F W F O W S L Q D L T B F
A Z R I Q M Z H X D S E Z R A N D Y R D J D H H Y U R P P
X O M G L I J P N K Y H E I K I R M W O O A C J M A B U H
C M B X F T X G Q C O M I T R W A R R S U N H W C C G A Q
W W Z K I D Q U S Q B F M Y S T R E L T S U H T U D W H S
T D U P S J U J G M W I B H O S P I T A L G I R X R D S B
A H K G J I U Q T S O Y Q R A N A P U E C D L D I A E V B
M N A P O O L S K I C F Y Z Y O C H H W R Y Q R Q N Y P T
B O T T L E T E M X S A L G U O D O B A K V I U O R J H J
F F L W X E V M X I H Q R R C I I G H P I X W J D E L O F
X G A X A S D G U A I V S V B I Q P F Q H X Y H Q B C Q A
G V W L E C F H I H I F F C V H E S G I O R D Q C T T K H
F P I S O T H R S I R G A L A H A D B D R U M I D S Z I D
G N B G Z Y G H X F D V B M S E S B M E K M K Z T B C D N
G F S A G O Y K S Z G Y R Y N Q A P T H M P N P W E E M B
```

AUTHORITY	DANCE	ST BERNARD	STEALING
BOTTLE	DOUGLAS	SIR GALAHAD	TIM
CAR	HOSPITAL	POOL	REFORMATORY
CORVETTE	HAIR	RANDY	TERRY JONES
COWBOY	HUSTLER	SOCS	SHEPHARD
CURLY	LION		

CROSSWORD *That Was Then, This Is Now*

CROSSWORD CLUES *That Was Then, This Is Now*

ACROSS
1 M&M and Cathy's last name
4 Told her friends to kill Mike
7 M&M wore this medallion
8 M&M's hippie nickname: Baby___
9 Mark cut her hair to get even for the fight
11 He was beaten for defending a black girl
12 Wanted to get even with Bryon and Mark
15 Leader of the Shepherd gang
18 Mark's car talent: Hot-___
19 Reason for Bryon's beating by the Shephards
20 Angela's and Curly's last name
21 Van-driving hippie college student
22 Bryon and Cathy's first date
24 Invited Bryon to their parties
26 Mark was selling them
28 Short; round; a real nut: ___Jones
30 Bryon's was in the hospital
31 Weapon used on Mark's head
32 Dirty ___ had brass knuckles
34 Saved Mark's and Bryon's lives
36 Bryon's pool talent
37 Tried to jump M&M
38 Bryon's last name

DOWN
1 Mark's real father
2 The kids drove up and down here
3 It was the same as buying, according to Mark
4 Bryon was given Charlie's
5 He looked like a friendly lion
6 Bryon did this a lot, according to Charlie
8 M&M's criticized his hair and grades
10 Mike described himself this way: Sir ___
11 He ran away from home
13 Bryon had never been able to accept it
14 Mark thought Mike was ___
16 Mark borrowed his car
17 Looked like a St. Bernard puppy
23 These riders made an obscene remark
25 M&M saw them on his bad trip
27 Mark resembled one
29 Mark's hippie nickname
31 Bryon thought he resembled one: St. ___
33 An innocent chick
35 Bryon's game

CROSSWORD *That Was Then, This Is Now*

MATCHING QUIZ/WORKSHEET 1 - That Was Then, This Is Now

___ 1. SPIDERS   A. Bryon's mother was here for a while

___ 2. TERRY   B. Bryon and Cathy's first date

___ 3. CONNIE   C. Short; round; a real nut: ___ Jones

___ 4. DOUGLAS   D. Angela and Curly's last name

___ 5. DANCE   E. Saved Mark's and Bryon's lives

___ 6. HOSPITAL   F. Mark thought Mike was ___

___ 7. STUPID   G. Mark borrowed his car

___ 8. LION   H. Bryon's game

___ 9. POOL   I. Tried to jump M&M

___ 10. SOCS   J. Wanted to get even with Bryon and Mark

___ 11. CHARLIE   K. Dirty ___ had brass knuckles

___ 12. MIKE   L. M&M's hippie nickname: Baby ___

___ 13. BERNARD   M. Told her friends to kill Mike

___ 14. PEACE   N. Invited Bryon to their parties

___ 15. CURLY   O. M&M wore this medallion

___ 16. FREAK   P. M&M saw them on his bad trip

___ 17. DAVE   Q. Bryon thought he resembled one: St. ___

___ 18. TEXANS   R. He was beaten for defending a black girl

___ 19. PRINCIPAL   S. Bryon's last name

___ 20. SHEPHARD   T. Mark resembled one

KEY: MATCHING QUIZ/WORKSHEET 1 - That Was Then, This Is Now

P - 1. SPIDERS   A. Bryon's mother was here for a while

C - 2. TERRY   B. Bryon and Cathy's first date

M - 3. CONNIE   C. Short; round; a real nut: ___ Jones

S - 4. DOUGLAS   D. Angela and Curly's last name

B - 5. DANCE   E. Saved Mark's and Bryon's lives

A - 6. HOSPITAL   F. Mark thought Mike was ___

F - 7. STUPID   G. Mark borrowed his car

T - 8. LION   H. Bryon's game

H - 9. POOL   I. Tried to jump M&M

N -10. SOCS   J. Wanted to get even with Bryon and Mark

E -11. CHARLIE   K. Dirty ___ had brass knuckles

R -12. MIKE   L. M&M's hippie nickname: Baby ___

Q -13. BERNARD   M. Told her friends to kill Mike

O -14. PEACE   N. Invited Bryon to their parties

I -15. CURLY   O. M&M wore this medallion

L -16. FREAK   P. M&M saw them on his bad trip

K -17. DAVE   Q. Bryon thought he resembled one: St. ___

J -18. TEXANS   R. He was beaten for defending a black girl

G -19. PRINCIPAL   S. Bryon's last name

D -20. SHEPHARD   T. Mark resembled one

MATCHING QUIZ/WORKSHEET 2 - That Was Then, This Is Now

___ 1. WIRING A. An innocent chick

___ 2. STEALING B. Short; round; a real nut: ___ Jones

___ 3. POOL C. Mark thought Mike was ___

___ 4. CORVETTE D. Mark's car talent: Hot-___

___ 5. TERRY E. Mark cut her hair to get even for the fight

___ 6. BERNARD F. He was beaten for defending a black girl

___ 7. COWBOY G. Bryon's game

___ 8. CURTIS H. Charlie used one to protect the boys

___ 9. CONNIE I. Bryon thought he resembled one: St. ___

___10. ANGELA J. M&M's hippie nickname: Baby ___

___11. CAR K. These riders made an obscene remark

___12. SHOTGUN L. Invited Bryon to their parties

___13. MIKE M. Bryon was given Charlie's

___14. DANCE N. Mark's real father

___15. STUPID O. Bryon's pool talent

___16. FREAK P. Bryon and Cathy's first date

___17. CATHY Q. He looked like a friendly lion

___18. SOCS R. Told her friends to kill Mike

___19. MARK S. It was the same as buying, according to Mark

___20. HUSTLER T. Unknowing object of Angela's affections

KEY: MATCHING QUIZ/WORKSHEET 2 - That Was Then, This Is Now

D - 1. WIRING   A. An innocent chick

S - 2. STEALING   B. Short; round; a real nut: ___ Jones

G - 3. POOL   C. Mark thought Mike was ___

K - 4. CORVETTE   D. Mark's car talent: Hot-___

B - 5. TERRY   E. Mark cut her hair to get even for the fight

I - 6. BERNARD   F. He was beaten for defending a black girl

N - 7. COWBOY   G. Bryon's game

T - 8. CURTIS   H. Charlie used one to protect the boys

R - 9. CONNIE   I. Bryon thought he resembled one: St. ___

E -10. ANGELA   J. M&M's hippie nickname: Baby ___

M -11. CAR   K. These riders made an obscene remark

H -12. SHOTGUN   L. Invited Bryon to their parties

F -13. MIKE   M. Bryon was given Charlie's

P -14. DANCE   N. Mark's real father

C -15. STUPID   O. Bryon's pool talent

J -16. FREAK   P. Bryon and Cathy's first date

A -17. CATHY   Q. He looked like a friendly lion

L -18. SOCS   R. Told her friends to kill Mike

Q -19. MARK   S. It was the same as buying, according to Mark

O -20. HUSTLER   T. Unknowing object of Angela's affections

WORD SCRAMBLE *That Was Then*

SCRAMBLE	WORD	CLUE
GNAEAL	ANGELA	Mark cut her hair to get even for the fight
THOYRIUTA	AUTHORITY	Bryon had never been able to accept it.
BYBKFAREA	BABY FREAK	M&M's hippie nickname
OETTBL	BOTTLE	weapon used on Mark's head
RYNOB	BRYON	looked like a Saint Bernard puppy
LANRCSO	CARLSON	M&M and Cathy's last name
AYTHC	CATHY	an innocent chick
HACRIEL	CHARLIE	saved Mark's and Bryon's lives
NONCIE	CONNIE	told her friends to kill Mike
VOTRCETE	CORVETTE	riders made an obscene remark
WYOCOB	COWBOY	Mark's real father
RLUCY	CURLY	tried to jump M&M
TUCISR	CURTIS	unknowing object of Angela's affections
ACEDN	DANCE	Bryon and Cathy's first date
SOULADG	DOUGLAS	Bryon's last name
THERFA	FATHER	M&M's criticized his hair and grades
SPLITHAO	HOSPITAL	Bryon's mother was here, for a while.
AHRI	HAIR	reason for Bryon's beating by the Shepherds
USTLREH	HUSTLER	Bryon's pool talent
OLNI	LION	Mark resembled one
AKMR	MARK	looked like a friendly lion
IKME	MIKE	beat up for defending a black girl
THERMO	MOTHER	Bryon's was in the hospital.
APCEE	PEACE	M&M wore this medallion.
ILPSL	PILLS	Mark was selling them.
RIAIPPLNC	PRINCIPAL	Mark 'borrowed' his car.
AYNDR	RANDY	van-driving hippie college student
NOIBBR	RIBBON	The kids drove up and down here.
EAPSHRHD	SHEPHARD	Angela and Curly's last name.
NOTSGHU	SHOTGUN	Charlie used one to protect the boys
PIERSSD	SPIDERS	M&M saw them on his bad trip
ESGTAINL	STEALING	it was the same as buying, according to Mark
READRBN	BERNARD	Bryon thought he resembled a St. __
DPITUS	STUPID	what Mark thought of Mike
XEASNT	TEXANS	wanted to get even with Bryon and Mark

VOCABULARY RESOURCES

VOCABULARY WORD SEARCH *That Was Then*

All of the words in this list are associated with *That Was Then, This Is Now* with emphasis on the vocabulary words being studied in the unit. The words are placed backwards, forward, diagonally, up and down. The clues below the word search will help identify the word.

```
V C O U Z R B K H X I A F C X T M I A H K L U N F G H Q
C O M M U N E U J N T X H S J Y B G D T N K O V C N O E
F T U B K Z G Z C S A C N F A L I F N V C H I F D I S A
E M C A L R H R P I E H G L G L H X Q G Q R G Z A T T T
F Q B I A S E R E N B S O C D A E K D C Z W Q C X N I J
Z X S V Z D P S D I A B E G E N H T G O C Y E F F U L Y
M L E A U J P V Z S N H E G N O Q B J A U R Z L K A I I
D L A L I A V Y Z T V G Y X Y I T E E H K A D W A T T W
Y E O C L F S R C E S I D K B T D Q U M R K A U E N Y F
A U S E I S R P K R M V X M G A I A I X G G M C L R K U
S A R P A R W E N G R D S Z P R D J E A P D K D O U Q Y
F D R S E D E N O I T N E M E R O F A L L S E R S X C E
O V F L V R J T N R C T B O T I N C K W P E U D P S C B
H Y X U C Q A L S Y L P H Z L E M A L D Z O C W W Q U M
R J V H R H B T L Y X P L G P W J T B H C B U L S S A R
V E N G E F U L E L H D M B I N D G F N G S B Z J B M Z
K A W G X D K B S L M N Q X F L N T J Y B Y I U D Q J V
Y L G N I G I L B O Y W Y Y M O S G D H L U W A B O D R
```

AFOREMENTIONED IRRATIONALLY SASSY
COMMUNE   LAME   SINISTER
DESPERATELY   LANKY   SLIGHT
GRAVELY   OBLIGINGLY   SOLE
HOSTILITY   PLEADING   TAUNTING
HYSTERICAL   RELAPSE   VENGEFUL
INCREDULOUS

VOCABULARY CROSSWORD *That Was Then, This Is Now*

VOCABULARY CROSSWORD CLUES *That Was Then, This Is Now*

ACROSS
1 Rude
3 Dealing with people in a skillful way
10 Moved in a bouncing or lively manner
11 Attack
14 Not logically
17 Conflict
21 Slipping back
23 Unclear
24 Joke
26 Said before
27 Wanting to give punishment for a wrong

DOWN
1 In a mocking manner
2 Threatening
3 Insulting; mean teasing
4 Twisted out of shape
5 Customs
6 Tall and skinny
7 Begging
8 Distance
9 Strolled
12 Willingly
13 Having an injured leg or foot
15 Suddenly
16 One who is under the legal age
17 In an uncontrolled, excitable state
18 Resolute
19 Supervised freedom for lawbreakers
20 Slowed
22 Light in form or build
25 Single; only

VOCABULARY CROSSWORD ANSWER KEY *That Was Then, This Is Now*

S	A	S	S	Y		T	A	C	T	F	U	L	L	Y	
A		I			A		O		O		A		P		G
R		N		S		U		N		R		N	F	L	O	U	N	C	E	D
C		I		A		N		T		M		K		E		L
A	S	S	A	U	L	T		O		A	Y			A	F			O
S		T		N		I		R		L		L		D			B
T		E		T		N		T	I	R	R	A	T	I	O	N	A	L	L	Y
I		R		E		G		E		T		M		N		B		I
C		R					D		I			E		G		R		G
A		E							E			M				U	
L		D			H	O	S	T	I	L	I	T	Y		P		N
L			P		S		Y			N		N			T		G
Y		R	E	L	A	P	S	E		T		O			L		L
		O		A		T			E		R		S	Y		Y
	O	B	S	C	U	R	E			N			L			
		A		K		R	W	I	T	T	I	C	I	S	M	
		T		E		I						G		M	S	
		I		D		C					H				O	
		O			A	F	O	R	E	M	E	N	T	I	O	N	E	D
	V	E	N	G	E	F	U	L							L	

146

VOCABULARY WORKSHEET 1 - That Was Then, This Is Now

___ 1. INCREDULOUS   A. Not logically

___ 2. GULF   B. Doubtful; disbelieving

___ 3. ABRUPTLY   C. Hopelessly

___ 4. HUB   D. Center

___ 5. MINOR   E. Conflict

___ 6. IRRATIONALLY   F. Resolute

___ 7. REMINISCING   G. Attack

___ 8. VAGUE   H. Begging

___ 9. ASSAULT   I. In an uncontrolled, excitable state

___10. FORMALITIES   J. Willingly

___11. LANKY   K. Distance

___12. INTENT   L. Slowed

___13. GRAVELY   M. Indistinct

___14. SLACKED   N. Seriously

___15. HYSTERICAL   O. Remembering past events

___16. HOSTILITY   P. One who is under the legal age

___17. OBLIGINGLY   Q. Tall and skinny

___18. PLEADING   R. Twisted out of shape

___19. CONTORTED   S. Customs

___20. DESPERATELY   T. Suddenly

KEY: VOCABULARY WORKSHEET 1 - That Was Then, This Is Now

B - 1. INCREDULOUS		A. Not logically
K - 2. GULF		B. Doubtful; disbelieving
T - 3. ABRUPTLY		C. Hopelessly
D - 4. HUB		D. Center
P - 5. MINOR		E. Conflict
A - 6. IRRATIONALLY		F. Resolute
O - 7. REMINISCING		G. Attack
M - 8. VAGUE		H. Begging
G - 9. ASSAULT		I. In an uncontrolled, excitable state
S - 10. FORMALITIES		J. Willingly
Q - 11. LANKY		K. Distance
F - 12. INTENT		L. Slowed
N - 13. GRAVELY		M. Indistinct
L - 14. SLACKED		N. Seriously
I - 15. HYSTERICAL		O. Remembering past events
E - 16. HOSTILITY		P. One who is under the legal age
J - 17. OBLIGINGLY		Q. Tall and skinny
H - 18. PLEADING		R. Twisted out of shape
R - 19. CONTORTED		S. Customs
C - 20. DESPERATELY		T. Suddenly

VOCABULARY WORKSHEET 2 - That Was Then, This Is Now

___ 1. SMIRKING   A. Joke

___ 2. SLIGHT   B. Twisted out of shape

___ 3. HYSTERICAL   C. Insulting; mean teasing

___ 4. AFOREMENTIONED D. Remembering past events

___ 5. HUB   E. Light in form or build

___ 6. IRRATIONALLY   F. In an uncontrolled, excitable state

___ 7. PROFOUND   G. Intellectual

___ 8. CONTORTED   H. Not logically

___ 9. ASSAULT   I. Distance

___10. RELAPSE   J. Said before

___11. LAME   K. Rude

___12. SASSY   L. Customs

___13. OBSCURE   M. Unclear

___14. SLACKED   N. Having an injured leg or foot

___15. WITTICISM   O. Sneering

___16. GULF   P. Slowed

___17. TAUNTING   Q. Center

___18. REMINISCING   R. Attack

___19. FORMALITIES   S. Willingly

___20. OBLIGINGLY   T. Slipping back

KEY: VOCABULARY WORKSHEET 2 - That Was Then, This Is Now

O - 1. SMIRKING	A. Joke
E - 2. SLIGHT	B. Twisted out of shape
F - 3. HYSTERICAL	C. Insulting; mean teasing
J - 4. AFOREMENTIONED	D. Remembering past events
Q - 5. HUB	E. Light in form or build
H - 6. IRRATIONALLY	F. In an uncontrolled, excitable state
G - 7. PROFOUND	G. Intellectual
B - 8. CONTORTED	H. Not logically
R - 9. ASSAULT	I. Distance
T - 10. RELAPSE	J. Said before
N - 11. LAME	K. Rude
K - 12. SASSY	L. Customs
M - 13. OBSCURE	M. Unclear
P - 14. SLACKED	N. Having an injured leg or foot
A - 15. WITTICISM	O. Sneering
I - 16. GULF	P. Slowed
C - 17. TAUNTING	Q. Center
D - 18. REMINISCING	R. Attack
L - 19. FORMALITIES	S. Willingly
S - 20. OBLIGINGLY	T. Slipping back

VOCABULARY WORD SCRAMBLE *That Was Then*

SCRAMBLE	**WORD**	**CLUE**
RPTAULYB	ABRUPTLY	suddenly
AAUSLST	ASSAULT	attack
MOMNCUE	COMMUNE	a group of people living together
DOTCORNTE	CONTORTED	twisted out of shape
FUNCOLDE	FLOUNCED	moved in a bouncing or lively manner
YARVGLE	GRAVELY	seriously
CDLIINNE	INCLINED	tending
ITETNN	INTENT	resolute
MALE	LAME	having an injured leg or foot
YANLK	LANKY	tall and skinny
NOIRM	MINOR	one who is under the legal age
EBCUSRO	OBSCURE	unclear
EGANDLPI	PLEADING	begging
OBPANTIOR	PROBATION	supervised freedom for lawbreakers
OUFODPNR	PROFOUND	intellectual
LAEPSER	RELAPSE	slipping back
RIISTNSE	SINISTER	threatening
KLADCSE	SLACKED	slowed
LIHTSG	SLIGHT	light in form or build
MNGIRKSI	SMIRKING	sneering
LOSE	SOLE	single; only
UALCTYTFL	TACTFULLY	dealing with people in a skillful way
NAGUNTTI	TAUNTING	insulting
AEGVU	VAGUE	indistinct
ELUNEVFG	VENGEFUL	wanting punishment for a wrong
SITICIWMT	WITTICISM	joke

www.ingramcontent.com/pod-product-compliance
Lightning Source LLC
Chambersburg PA
CBHW051411070526
44584CB00023B/3378